Please remember that this is a library book,
and that it belongs only temporarily to each
person who uses it. Be considerate. Do
not write in this, or any, library book.

How to Release
the Learning Power
in Children

How to Release
the Learning Power
in Children

AUGUSTA GOLDIN

PARKER PUBLISHING COMPANY, INC.
West Nyack, N.Y.

PRINTED IN THE UNITED STATES OF AMERICA

ISBN 0-13-430876-X
B&P

To Oscar and Rae

How This Book Can
Assist Teachers

This book concentrates on educational action. It describes teaching methods that insure effective learning and spells out practical ideas that have been tested in situations like your own.

Planning, as any experienced teacher knows, is the vital key. It is possible, however, to plan skillfully in terms of your class, your subject matter, your materials of instruction, and implement carefully in terms of the community and the times, only to find that solid, functional learning eludes your children. There are times when you may experience some wonderful happenings in your classroom, with, here and there, some remarkable social development. You may also experience considerable dismay at the end of the school year, when you find that required basics, mandated by the local school board, have been covered only in part. It is even possible that many children will fail to progress noticeably in arithmetic, in written English, in reading skills; and you may find that a few standard scores have, unaccountably, dropped.

Low scores, partial achievement, and slow progress are

symptoms of *limited learning,* and we know that this sometimes happens because many children do not learn what the teacher believes she is teaching.

This book analyzes the symptoms of limited learning in terms of their causes, which are real and identifiable. It explores ways of eliminating these causes, and shows how to prevent their recurrence. It also indicates practical approaches: for planning key activities; and for making these plans work for you.

In this book, new ideas point the way: HOW-TO set up an environment for learning that *releases the learning power of children* is backed up with the HOW-TO of *equipping children with the skills they need,* so they can capitalize on this released learning power. HOW-TO effect a well-paced balance of exciting *learning activities* is backed up with the HOW-TO of *direct teaching skills,* so as to insure guided learning. HOW-TO maintain *continuous progress* and nail it down is backed up with the HOW-TO of *helping children make use of their learning,* consciously and constructively.

For the best of us there is little time to lose.

Elementary school children receive fewer than 6,000 hours of instruction in Grades 1 through 6. In these 6,000 hours they are expected to learn the three *R*'s in depth, the study skills in meaningful context, and functional techniques for independent study. They are expected to achieve high level social competence in group activities. They are expected to develop all-around constructive behavior patterns.

And these are not unrealistic expectations.

The cultural community looks to us for an educated, literate citizenry.

Business looks to us for personnel capable of functioning in the business world.

Parents want college-bound children.

Taxpayers want their money's worth.

And no one wants these things more than the teacher!

So—let us recognize, isolate and overcome the causes of limited learning.

And the objective of this book is to focus on practical approaches that will help us do precisely that!

Augusta Goldin

Contents

Contents

CONTENTS

sonality • One Easy Way to Write Up a Behavior Record •
Scholastic Records Are Only Ratings

Devise class records that work

Four Steps in Checking Add Up to a Progress Record • Progress Record Techniques Apply to All Curriculum Areas

Encourage children's records that work for them
Children's Planning Records

10 Increasing Parental Cooperation • 207

Cooperation is a joint operation that involves understanding • *Operation understanding is achieved in two steps*

One Way to Synchronize Teachers' Aims and Parents' Aims • One Way to Establish Communication That Communicates What You Want to Say

Guidelines for effective communication with parents

You Will Need a 9 to 3 Forcefield Around Your Classroom of "There-Shall-Be-No's" • You Will Need Parental Involvement in Devising This Communication System, Meaning • A Class Meeting of Parents Will Communicate the Class Program to Parents • The Individual Conference with Parents Will Consider the Progress of Individual Children

Now you know

11 Applying Regular Evaluation to Insure Continued Learning • 225

This was a good year

Evaluation? You Need a Double Base! • The Average Teaching Day Is a Three-Way Day • Methods Structure Your Lessons! • Eight Lessons Constitute a Structured Series • Success Formula for Educational Action

Index • 247

How to Release
the Learning Power
in Children

1

Organizing the Classroom as a
Laboratory for Discovery

This is going to be a good year

This is going to be a good year.
You have familiarized yourself with the course of study. You
know the work you will be required to cover. And you have
a pretty good idea of grouping for pinpointed needs and
creative expansion.

You'll have nothing to do but teach! And so you come
to school two or three days before class starts, to write up
your planbook. You unlock your door and you are appalled.

Your room looks like a barracks. The closets are bulging
with books and supplies. Furniture is stacked in the middle
of the floor, and you can't even find your chair. Only the
shades are neatly drawn, subtle declaration to the community
that this is a neat and tidy school.

Your room is clean, scrubbed and painted. That's about
all it is.

"When I went to school," you say to yourself, "our
classroom was beautiful. There was a place for everything
and everything was in its place."

Within two days, your room will be beautiful, too. It

will also be a place to live in and work in. More, it will be so geared to learning that it will virtually serve as a Laboratory for Discovery.

A laboratory for discovery in five easy steps

All you need is a plan, and here's one that works in five easy steps.

STEP 1—GET HELP

Three or four tireless youngsters are best. Call some mothers, borrow their children, and make friends for life.

STEP 2—PUT YOUR ROOM TO RIGHTS

Shove the furniture into place and *count*. You need a table and chair for each child on your register. You also need three tables for displays, five or six chairs for study circles, and two chairs for visitors. If you are short, call on your principal, but put your needs in writing so that he may approve your request and route it to the janitor. If your principal isn't available, leave your written request in his mailbox. Be specific when you ask for things: say so many 26-inch tables, so many small or middle sized chairs, so many visitor's chairs. Be insistent if your request is not filled in a reasonable length of time. Be firm. If it doesn't work, be ingenious and make do with what you have.

STEP 3—CHECK FOR MISCELLANEOUS ROOM FURNISHINGS

Do you have a flag and a bulletin board? An easel, a fish tank, a pencil sharpener and a stapler? Do you have a waste basket, a box of chalk and board rubbers? Place these things where they belong in your room. List missing items on a "Wanted" list, and for the time being, hold your peace. They may show up later when you go through your closets. If they don't, then you will ask for them.

So much for the room, which by this time looks almost habitable. Only 30 minutes have passed, the whole day stretches ahead, and your inexhaustible helpers are just getting into stride. So. . . .

STEP 4—LOCATE YOUR BOOK INVENTORY

As soon as you have located your book inventory, prepare to check your supplies against it. You will find this inventory in your desk or filed away in the office. If you can't locate it, take inventory from scratch. You must know what materials you have to work with, if you are to plan your work intelligently.

Taking inventory or checking inventory is neither easy nor hard, only necessary. You simply have to organize yourself and the things that are jammed into your closets, and you will be done before you know it. If you have to take inventory from scratch, make it easy for yourself. Note the books in each subject area, and make your notations on two forms like those in Figures 1 and 2.

As you check out your books, reference materials and other supplies, you'll be surprised at the diversity of things that have been issued to you. You'll see that the average classroom easily contains about $1,500 worth of educational materials, with more sets of books in the upper grades, and more dolls, toys, puzzles and expensive play equipment in the lower grades.

All these things fall into two categories, the verbal and the non-verbal—a good thing to remember when you take inventory.

Begin your inventory of the verbal things

Start with the texts and workbooks, reference materials, maps and globes.

Locate your globes. Get them dusted and set up on top of your clothing closet.

Examine your maps. Make certain they are suitable for your grade and that the rollers work. Now hang them up in front of your room.

Inventory of Class Texts and Reference Materials
for Class_____

Subject Area	Grade Level	Title	Publisher	Number on Hand
LANGUAGE ARTS				
Basic Readers				
Supplementary Readers				
Literature Books				
Skills Materials				
Thesauri				
Dictionaries				
SOCIAL STUDIES				
Texts				
Encyclopedias				
Atlas				
Almanac				
Maps				
Globes				
MATHEMATICS				
SCIENCE				
HEALTH				
MUSIC				
ART				
Readers				
Folios				

Figure 1

Look around for your class library books which are probably tied up in a couple of cartons. Get them sorted into
library categories: fiction and non-fiction, how-to books, biographies and miscellaneous. Stack them into one of your
bookcases and glue a sticker, appropriately labeled, above
each category.

Find your reference materials: encyclopedias and dic-

Inventory of Class Library Books
for Class_____

Classification	Title	Publisher	Number on Hand
Fiction			
Science Fiction			
Tall Tales			
General Non-Fiction			
Biographies			
Autobiographies			
Miscellaneous			

Figure 2

tionaries, atlases, world almanacs and thesauri, and stack them in another bookcase. You may not have all of these materials, or you may have more or you may have less. Organize whatever you have, for easy use.

You have now made a sizable dent in your closets, at the same time that you have arranged the books which belong in the bookcases. The day is still young, but checking out your texts and workbooks will take considerable time. So take a break and chat with your helpers.

You chat about the areas you are going to study in this grade. Social studies? Yes, and language arts, math, science, health, music and art. Seven areas! Make a small sign for each of these areas, drop a sign on every fourth table, and get those books out of your closets and onto the proper tables.

Sort the books by subject area first, then stack them

according to title. Remember to keep companion texts together with the workbooks and teacher's manuals. As soon as that is done, collect one of each title for your own use, for your own desk. Then return your sorted books to the closets in such a way that they will be available for instant use by the children—each set visible when the closet door is opened, all titles front, and right side up.

You may find you have so many books that you face a storage problem. Don't ask to have them removed from your room. They may not be available when you develop a burning need for them at some later date. Anyway, your children will be using some of these books at home, and keeping some in their desks, so your storage problem will erase itself.

On the other hand, you may find that you are short and will be expected to share books with your colleagues. Sharing is often a built-in policy, even in the best schools, where one set of books is provided for an entire grade, in the so-called minor subjects. If, then, you find no health, or music or science books in your room, check with the teacher next door. If it's sharing you have to do, share, but rule out interruptions that may blow a lesson. Share only on specified days. Use only two assigned and carefully instructed monitors. Move the books only before the school bell rings.

If you find, after your books are back in the closets and after you have consulted with your colleagues, that you need additional books, either to complete a given set or a given subject area, make a note of your needs on your "Wanted" list. Again, be specific! Ask for so many books in math or science; indicate the title and publisher and grade level. Hold this list for two or three days so that you can indicate additional needs, then place it in your principal's mailbox. And be patient. You are not the only one in the building needing things, and you don't need everything on your list the first week of school.

You have now completed a major chore and it's time for lunch.

Continue your inventory of non-verbal things

After lunch, and some good, useful talk in the teachers' lunchroom, look through your non-verbal supplies. Many of these are expendable, so you need not bother with a formal inventory.

You may find a plethora of supplies, including vast stores of science materials and balls and games for health education, or you may find that your cupboards are bare. No matter, you need only a minimum to get started with:

- two or three reams of ruled and unruled paper
- three or four red marking pencils
- scotch tape
- thumb tacks
- out-of-the-room pass
- colored construction paper and some basic jars of paint and newsprint
- math materials—rulers and measuring cups and, if you can get them, bead frames, magna boards, scales, graph paper and tape measures.

If you don't have these things, scrounge! Borrow from your colleagues (but be sure to pay back later), and enlist the aid of your children. Just convince them that the class needs their efforts, and in no time you will truly have a storage problem.

Now arrange the expendable supplies in one of your closets. You'll have more room, then, for the largesse the central office will be sending you in short order.

At this point, you may rest on your laurels or you may not. You may say, "What a job, taking inventory, reorganizing the closets and putting the room to rights." It is. It is a tremendous job. But already your room has all the earmarks of a good workshop, and that's splendid.

You have now completed four of the five easy steps in the plan to organize your classroom for learning. But the best planned workshop will not *stimulate* learning in children. If they come into a static, well organized situation, they will respond in a static, well organized manner, because children like to please and they will mirror your ways. It will be harder to quicken curiosity and ignite enthusiasm later, if you have to work against the apathy and intellectual inertia that was set the first day.

It's now time for the last step in your plan to turn the classroom into a Laboratory for Discovery.

Step 5—Display Premeditated Attractions

Seven tempting areas in your classroom will do it, and all seven should be set up before the children report to school. For your children, these areas will spell opportunity for acquiring the learnings you want them to acquire. They also spell delight because of the built-in opportunities for self-discovery.

With unquestioned sincerity, a colleague may counsel you to leave your room as it is. "Give the children a chance to fix it up. Wait till they get into their units. The classroom belongs to them!"

The classroom belongs to all of you, yourself included. True, you are only one, but you are a very important one, and you have two days before school starts to set the tone in your room.

Set it, and avoid weeks of barren surroundings, false starts, wasted materials, and bruising frustration. Show them a model of a challenging environment. Show them a Lab for Discovery, and in short order they will replace your seven efforts with overflowing evidences of their own learning discoveries.

To activate a Lab for Discovery, you need one day, a good plan, and those seven areas.

You will indeed need a good plan to contrive seven display areas in your four-cornered room. So make a start this afternoon and finish up tomorrow. Begin with:

Area #1—Set up your Library Corner around the bookcases. Since it's autumn, highlight harvest scenes, seasonal poems and an account of Labor Day in strategically opened books. Invite surprise with a bowl of speckled corn and dried out gourds from the 5 and 10¢ store.

Area #2—For your Math Corner, use a small table laid out with common measuring instruments: assorted rulers, measuring cups and spoons and a small scale. Post a neatly lettered question above the table: WHAT KIND OF DRY THINGS AND WHAT KIND OF WET THINGS CAN THESE INSTRUMENTS MEASURE?

Area #3—Your Science Area may center around the fish tank. Challenge the children with a provocative question: WHY DON'T THESE FISH DROWN? And, if you can get them, also display two branches: one with the leaves turning color; the other, an all green evergreen. Display, too, a one word question, WHY?

Area #4—Back your Social Studies Area right up against the rear wall of your room, and base it on current events. If you have an upper grade, post or draw a 3' x 4' map of the world on the board, with strings running from the major countries to the table below. Anchor the strings in lumps of clay and place each lump on a library card. The library card will serve to keep the table clean, and will provide space for the answer to the caption that you've boldly printed above the map. The caption? TAKE ME TO YOUR LEADER. And you'll be launching your class on current events with a focus!

If, however, your children are very young, your social studies area may develop around the family. Arrange assorted cut-outs or pictures of boys and girls and men and women on a flannel board, and hang your board on the wall. On the table beneath it, place library cards (backed with bits of flannel so they may later adhere to your board). On each library card, have one word, neatly printed. Each word should indicate some familial relationship, so you will want to be prepared with *ME, MOTHER, FATHER, AUNT, UNCLE, NIECE, NEPHEW, GRANDMOTHER, GRANDFATHER, COUSIN.*

On the first day that you meet your class, you will be able to find out much about your children as they introduce their families to you. And on the second day they can begin making up their own family cut-outs, prelude to your social studies unit!

Area #5—The Art Corner is very easy to arrange. Place your easel near the sink. If you have no sink, place it in a far corner, away from traffic. Get two tall coffee cans: one for brushes, one for water. You also need two or three jars of paint, a few sheets of newsprint fastened to the easel with two clothespins, and a square of linoleum or heavy brown paper to catch the drips.

Area #6—Your Music Area will lift the emotional tone of your room. Show off your rhythm band instruments for younger children—your melody bells, flutes, recorders and music records for older children. If you have no equipment of this kind, make a big thing of pictures showing musicians performing, vocally or with the aid of instruments. Top this picture display with such questions as:

- Have you heard . . . ?
- Do you like . . . ?

Area #7—The corner focusing on a Center of Interest may turn out to be the heartbeat of your class. Here you may display figures or dolls if you can borrow them from the local museum (if not, fall back on pictures) of the Hero of the Month.

Should you have doubts about your students' attitudes toward conventional heroes, post pictures of dog heroes, or save this idea for a later day and start with proverbs. Choose half a dozen proverbs that are suitable to the age of your children. Write these proverbs in color on 6 x 9 sheets of oaktag and post them on the cork panels of your wardrobe closets. You will be well into your language arts when you ask your children to do one of three things:

- Accept the proverbs as written.
- Paraphrase them.
- Update them.

How, for example, might they paraphrase or update these common sayings?

Speak softly and carry a big stick.
. . . Who fights with sticks in the cities today?

Time and tide wait for no man.
. . . When we have broken the sound barrier?

A stitch in time saves nine.
. . . What would happen to our economy if we discarded our policy of built-in obsolescence?

Waste not, want not.
. . . What about the government's insistence that farmers plow under their crops?

Many hands make light work.
. . . What hands in this age of automation?

A new broom sweeps clean.
. . . How many children have never seen a broom— only mops and vacuum cleaners?

It takes two to make a quarrel.
. . . Does it? What about unprovoked attacks?

What you don't know won't hurt you!
. . . It won't?

Finally, your seven areas are set up. Finally, everything is in place. Your room looks beautiful, warm, and welcoming, and powered for learning. You've done a professional job.

There's nothing to do now, but look forward to welcoming the class tomorrow.

Actually, there is one more thing to do before you meet your class, and that is to set up and use your bulletin board as an open sesame for belonging. So far, you've only displayed your materials of instruction. Now display a human factor. Be personal. Involve your children. Take a moment

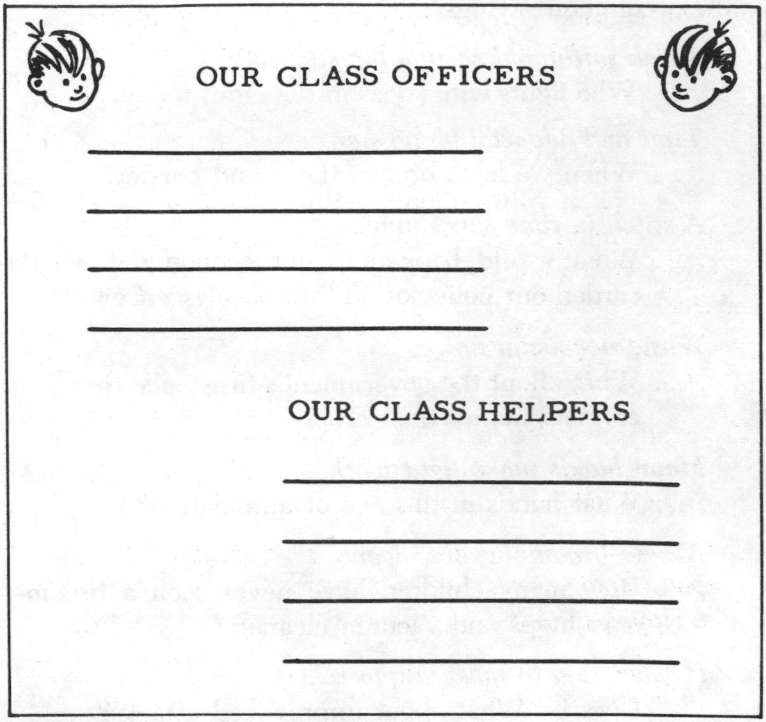

OUR CLASS OFFICERS

OUR CLASS HELPERS

Figure 3

to tack brightly colored letters on your bulletin board which communicate their message clearly and look like this. (*Figure 3*).

Within a few days, the children, under your guidance,

will determine the number and kind of officers and helpers they need. And they will do this in a democratic and participatory activity.

And at last, tomorrow, the first day of school finally arrives. You've made a last minute check of your syllabi and manuals, and you've drawn up a detailed one-day plan.

Now your children are at the door. The line is straight, the faces scrubbed. All are under tight control. Two or three eye you cautiously. One sports a speculative gleam.

You say, "Good morning boys and girls," and the school year has begun.

It's touch and go

You look at your children and you wonder, "Will I ever be able to mold *them* into a cohesive group?"

And your children look at you and wonder, "*What is she like?*"

. . . *Maybe she's not so bad. She's got pictures of children on the wall. She must like children.* (And you get a second speculative glance.)

. . . *Things to play with! Fish and speckled corn! I think I'll like it, here.*

. . . *Paper under the easel. That means she* expects *paint spots on the floor. It might just be O.K. here, for a Sloppy Joe like me.*

. . . *She's going to let us be officers and helpers. I'd like to be one of those.*

Yes, you will mold them into a cohesive group

You look at their faces and you read them. Yes, you will be able to mold them into a cohesive group of individuals, and they will make good use of your Lab for Discovery. They'll learn, and it won't matter a bit whether they are bright or slow, primary children or upper graders. If they are bright, you will work them hard and at a good tempo, and you will be very particular about particulars. If they are slow and retarded in reading, you will nevertheless not slacken your pace. You will merely change direction and move them onto another track of learning—the track of more direct experiences: of trips and excursions, audio-visuals, interviews, projects and exhibits. Kept at a good tempo, and permitted satisfaction by way of direct experiences, your slow students will soon feel the need for greater depth in learning. They will be stung by their reading inadequacies and will determine to read. You will then have few problems teaching them as individuals, as small groups, or as a class. And then, any method will do.

But this will come later.

Now, your job is to mold these children into a cohesive, working entity, and you will do it in three ways:

1. You will share with them the planning and development of your goals, which are also the goals of your community. Then they will understand that school is more than a place in which they put in time.

2. You will share with them the contents of your book inventory. They need to know, as well as you do, what materials of instruction are available to them in the seven areas of the curriculum. They also need to know where they can obtain special information in a hurry; for example that the address of the current World Fair can be located in an atlas, the batting average of players in an almanac, and a true account of moon probes in an encyclopedia.

3. You will share with them ways of determining common goals and individual interests, as well as ways of developing these goals and interests.

And your children, in turn, will share with you the responsibility of seeing that Number 3 above prevails in the classroom.

It will take time to do this kind of molding, so you begin immediately, and Chapter 2 will show you how.

Yes—this is going to be a good year.

2

Involving Children in Sharing Responsibilities

Occasionally you meet up with another teacher, brightly enthusiastic and highly professional, who tells you that her children made up a class newspaper, produced a play, and set up an award winning exhibit. "And I had nothing to do with it. They did it all themselves!"

Such a teacher is either unduly modest or totally unaware of her own skill, because such high-level, ongoing, responsible learning activities simply do not happen without the supportive guidance of a skillful teacher.

A responsible group is a cohesive group

For children to perform as a responsible, producing group, they must first be a *cohesive* group, and this means that three operating conditions exist:

- They share a common purpose.
- They hold themselves responsible for a set of class-formulated ground rules.

35

- They seek, accept and thrive on learnings that will further their common purpose.

In such a cohesive group, children can indeed make up a newspaper, produce a play, and set up an exhibit. Children can do almost anything if they want to, provided they receive directional guidance. At one and the same time, they can exhibit enormous proclivities for work; they can muster tremendous potential for understanding; but they can also display unbelievable ignorance of the simplest facts.

Your job is to release this potential by replacing their basic ignorance with learning skills.

This will take time, so you begin right away.

A cohesive group needs ground rules

Your Lab for Discovery will serve as home base. Your children will serve as the players. What you need now is a triple set of ground rules covering:

- safety routines,
- the economical use of time,
- the intelligent use of learning sources.

And then, full steam ahead for learning the learning skills.

It would be simple indeed to write the ground rules on the board and tell your children, "This is the way we do things in this room." Don't! If you tell them, they won't hear you. If you are a strong disciplinarian, they will soon learn it's wise to please you, and will memorize, verbatim, the rules *you* propounded. But they won't buy your rules and they won't become a cohesive group.

ADD A LIBERAL DASH OF MIRACLE I

The cement that binds a cohesive group is Miracle I, the "I" standing for Involvement of Children. So involve them. Set up a situation, and, adding a dash of Miracle I, start by asking about ground rules instead of announcing them. Guide your children in formulating the rules that you know are necessary for cohesive living. Use your chalkboard, and on it write:

Problem 1: *Do we need any rules in this class?*

    Yes?
    No?
    Why?

Imperceptibly, your children will recoil at the word *rules.* If, however, you say little and listen pleasantly, they will soon begin to speak freely:

- We need rules so there won't be any fighting.
- We need rules to keep us out of trouble.
- We need rules to keep us (ugh!) good, so we can go on trips.
- (And with tongue in cheek) We need rules so we can learn.

How true! And so you write again on the chalkboard:

Problem 2: *What rules would you consider suitable for this class?*

You will almost be able to hear the shifting of mental gears, before the discussion quickens and spills over. The children will make suggestions that are sound and wild, utopian and grim. You write them all down on the board, noting next to each suggestion the name of the child who made it. This will give immediate status to the contributors, and will provide you later with names for committee assignments.

When the discussion runs down, your board will be filled up. All sorts of binders will now be indicated, ranging from the use of the pencil sharpener, to ways of hanging up wraps; from the need for exact change for milk-money, to the borrowing of class library books.

"All those rules for this one class!" you say in amazement, and this only invites more discussion. Cut it short.

You have a score of suggestions, all enthusiastically proffered by individuals. These suggestions need to be trimmed down and accepted by the class.

Help the class lump similar suggestions together, and you will find them falling into three categories spelled out in the rough, for safety routines, the economical use of time, and the wise use of learning sources.

Now, Rome wasn't built in a day, so provide a change of pace, and stop for another dash of Miracle I. Appoint a Ground Rules Committee for each of the three categories on your board. Charge each committee to develop its own category in terms of these four helpful hints:

- List no more than six good rules.
- Make the rules practical and fair.
- Write the rules in such a way that there will be no misunderstandings and no arguments from the legal eagles.
- Be prepared to revise your rules if the class has better ideas.

Then, in order to build status and recognition into the committees, and to routinize your own working habits:

- Write the titles of your committees on a chart.
- Indicate, under each of these titles, the names of the committee members, making it a point to star the name of the chairman.
- Note the date clearly on which each of these committees is due to report to the class.

You look about you then, and yes, you're on the way to molding a cohesive group. You've begun your first teaching day with such a strong dash of Miracle I that already you have 12 children assigned to committees.

Now, if the warning bells aren't ringing in your head, they should be, because for children, there's a vast difference between *being* committee members, and *functioning* as committee members. Unless you provide some preparatory help, each child faces frustration, each committee will fall apart, and then no amount of Miracle I will restore today's confident enthusiasm.

AVOID DISASTER AND INSURE SUCCESS

You have to assume that your committees need instruction in procedure. Certainly, after a long summer vacation, even the best trained children need to review committee practices. Since these are not academic committees (the kind that are charged with the heavy artillery of research and pooling), helping them should be a fairly simple matter. But don't brake your entire class to a stop so that you can instruct 12 children. Set up a committee meeting time, say 20 minutes before school starts the next day, and then, with the formality and attention due important committees, help them.

Clarify Committee Responsibilities

Question: What are the duties of a chairman?

Answer: To call meetings, to keep the discussion going and to keep the members to the point.

Question: What are the duties of the committee members?

Answer 1: One member must serve as a secretary and take notes in a notebook.

Answer 2: One must serve as a board-writer and write notes on the board when necessary. He must write neatly and make sure that he spells correctly and uses periods and capitals properly. That's so that we can make sense out of his notes.

Answer 3: All committee members have to work together to make up a solid report for the class.

Question: How does a committee report to the class?

Answer 1: The board-writer writes the name of the committee and the names of all the members on the board *before* school starts. He also writes any notes that the committee considers important.

Answer 2: At reporting time, the entire committee sits at a table in front of the room, with dignity and importance. The report may be given by the chairman or by each of the members. Then the committee answers questions raised by the class.

Review Procedures for Reporting

It's a good idea, especially at the beginning of the term, to meet again with each committee just before reporting time in order to review simple reporting procedures. Don't permit children to fail if you can help it. They learn infinitely more from success.

A cohesive group begins to take shape

And then the day finally comes, when Committee #1, on safety routines, is due to report to the class.

COMMITTEE 1 FORMULATES GROUND RULES FOR SAFETY ROUTINES

Committee 1 is ready. With commendable pride, the children present the six items they consider most important, and these are:

1. Observe one-way traffic when your line goes to or from the coat closet.

2. Keep your books in your desk, and your lunch, if you have any, in the closet. The floor is not for storage.

3. Keep all feet under the desk, and keep them on the floor.

4. Seats are for sitting in, not for stretching in. And don't wander around the room.

5. Walk on the stairs. Don't run and don't fool around. Take one step at a time, and never go backwards.

6. Freeze when you hear the fire gongs. Then, if you're out of your seat, go to it quickly, and your row will be called for line-up.

These six items just about cover the safety front. You could hardly do better yourself.

Any discussion?

Encourage it. Encourage questions and objections so that the class can thrash out this entire area of behavior that goes with school safety, and make it their own. Watch your children as they participate, and watch your time. If you allow too little time, the topic will be covered, but not developed. If you allow too much, the children will get restless. Five or ten minutes for this sort of discussion is more than enough for little children. Older ones can keep a discussion going profitably for 20 minutes or more. And throughout this discussion, the committee will explain the rules in detail, defend them soundly, and modify them if need be.

Does the class accept these rules?

With slight modifications, the class accepts the rules, and the committee is instructed to print up a large chart, titled A CODE OF BEHAVIOR FOR SAFETY'S SAKE FOR OUR CLASS.

The committee will feel ten feet tall when they complete the chart and you post it conspicuously.

And for the rest of the year, you hold them to it!

In this one area of safety, your class has now experienced two of the three operating conditions that characterize a cohesive group:

- the shared purpose;
- the class formulated rules.

The experiencing of the third condition, the quest for academic learning, is still some distance in the future.

In the meantime, keep building responsible status. Arrange for an election of officers and make certain that the qualifications are spelled out clearly and in advance. Assign housekeeping committees, and then post all the names on the bulletin board.

COMMITTEE 2 FORMULATES GROUND RULES FOR THE ECONOMICAL USE OF TIME

And now, Committee 2 is pushing its way into the limelight. Having met with you previously, the committee members are certain that they have picked your brains, and accordingly, are bursting with the word on how to use time to best advantage. The board-writer can hardly wait to chalk up his tantalizing caption on the board:

HOW TO SAVE ONE DAY A MONTH
FOR OUR OWN (?) PURPOSES!

And this committee proposes six solid rules, the observance of which is calculated to save the class one day's worth of time, a mere 300 minutes, every month of the year.

Rules	Time Saved in One Month
1. Save time at the pencil sharpener. Don't even use it in class. Bring two sharpened pencils from home every day. This will save at least five minutes a day, or 25 minutes a week, which adds up to 100 minutes a month	100 minutes
2. Don't fool around in the coat closet. This will save another five minutes a day	100 minutes
3. Save two minutes a day when you pass your test papers forward by putting *your* paper on top. When your papers are returned, take yours off the top. Two minutes × five days × four weeks is 40 minutes saved a month	40 minutes

4. Have correct change on the day when you bring in milk or lunch money. If the teacher has to make change for you, *she* wastes time, about ten minutes a week. So bring in the exact amount of money you're supposed to, and save another 40 minutes a month ....40 minutes

5. Put your books away as soon as you come into the room, but put your homework on your desk, ready to be checked by the teacher. Save five minutes of class time a day, every day ....100 minutes

6. And make up your mind to do things right the first time. We can't even figure how much time you'd save this way, but it would be a lot.

The committee indicates a saving of 380 minutes a month—more than six hours—more than a whole school day. And they are being conservative. Double that figure or triple it, and you will come closer to the time that is frittered away in aimless activity every month. And, with this loss, there's a slow-down of interest as youthful energies go underground for purposes of fooling around, pretending attention and contriving mischief. And what about you, then? What happens to your great feelings of achievement? Gone! Dissipated in righteous scolding and nagging and prodding.

Don't, however, permit overemphasis on the mechanics of time-saving. You know that all children need some time for unstructured living, even in the classroom, and your immature children need even more.

But—right now, what does Committee 2 propose to do with that saved day?

Committee 2 has a plan. And this plan dovetails with the plan of Committee 3!

COMMITTEE 3 FORMULATES GROUND RULES
FOR THE INTELLIGENT USE OF LEARNING SOURCES

Committee 3 is very businesslike. It is, after all, easy to understand that one learns from many sources. It is also easy to understand that we learn in different ways.

Notes for this report, placed on the board by the committee's board-writer before school starts, may look like this:

What We Learn from	How We Learn
1. Printed things: books and maps, magazines, newspapers and comic books.	By reading.
2. Pictures, charts and graphs.	By figuring out the meanings.
3. TV and radio, records and tapes.	By watching and listening.
4. Making things: model planes or cars, doll dresses, cookies; putting on plays and exhibits.	By following directions and using our heads and our hands and working together.
5. People: teachers, parents, friends, firemen, policemen, telephone workers, mechanics, and even people who don't work.	By listening and asking questions.
6. Places: museums, parks, libraries, zoos, schools and historical landmarks.	By going on trips and excursions.

It's a good report. Committee 3 has learned to present the results of its thinking in a straightforward manner (thanks to your preparatory meetings), and the class is with them.

You glow over Item 4. So—they sense that learning takes place from making up plays and exhibits! But more water will have to flow under the bridge before the learning skills necessary to the completion of such projects are theirs. But soon—soon—it won't be long now.

You tell Committee 3 the report was good; in fact, quite comprehensive. They included virtually all the learning sources when they included people and places and things.

But what of the saved day that Committee 2 noted so mysteriously? And why is the class looking at you so expectantly?

"That's it," the children inform you. "The places and people! The trips. We can go on a trip once a month to any place, because the saved day is ours!"

It's obvious that the whole class was privy to this planned reasoning. It was a secret, solidly kept, to surprise you at the proper moment.

A cohesive group is realized

When a class, after working together only two or three weeks, has learned to practice this kind of cohesive behavior—you deserve congratulations! You've attained the rank of *pro*.

Now work at it!

The first order of business is to get committees assigned to explore special one-day trip possibilities.

If the children are young, they will want to explore the neighborhood because they live in a world of here-and-now. If the children are older, they will want to go farther afield and behind the scenes.

And they will continue to need your guiding hand in planning the trip, and in following up the learnings growing out of the trip.

What a lot of enthusiasm you have released in your class!

TRANSLATE ENTHUSIASM INTO LEARNING POWER

To translate this enthusiasm, preplan two learning activities involving interview techniques and business letter skills. And with these two activities, your social studies program will take on new dimensions.

It may take a week or two before your class is ready to consider and profit from interview techniques or business letter skills. And to an untrained observer, your development at that time of these two learning activities will seem like happy incidentals. To a pro, nothing that happens in the classroom is incidental.

And this is the way in which your children will now move ahead from enthusiastic planning to satisfying achievement.

If yours is a primary grade and it's the neighborhood that's going to be explored, the class must first have some general idea of *what* they are going to explore and *how* they are going to do it.

Start by defining the neighborhood as the place where their neighbors live. This may be the area that extends approximately five blocks from the school in each of the four directions: eastward toward the rising sun, westward toward the setting sun, northward as indicated by the compass, and southward. Then do a little homework yourself. Walk around the neighborhood and check out the learning possibilities in this square. No matter where your school is located, in the country, the suburbs, or the inner city, you will find that a neighborhood is made up of different kinds of buildings which serve different kinds of purposes for the people in it.

And so, in planning this trip, you ask your class, "What kind of places might we see on this neighborhood walk?"

And the children will tell you:

- Houses that people live in.
- Stores and factories that people work in.
- Movies and theatres and bowling alleys that people have fun in.
- Beauty parlors that ladies get pretty in. (And barber shops for men.)

- Buildings that city workers work in: policemen, postmen, firemen, tax collectors.
- Hospitals that people get well in.
- Garages and dental offices that things get fixed in.
- Also empty buildings and maybe bridges and train stations.

Such a long list of buildings in the neighborhood! Now rexograph it and illustrate it with very simple sketches for the benefit of those children whose reading is below par. Then each child gets a copy of this rexographed list for his notebook, and off you go on your neighborhood trip.

Some of the items listed may not exist in your area. On the other hand, you may be able to make exciting discoveries: an animal hospital, a Chinese grocery, a pizzeria, an ice cream stand, a bank, a cobbler's shop, a German bakery, a photographer's studio—and all these are added by the children to their list of places in the neighborhood.

But a list is only a list. With little effort, you and the children could have developed such a list of places merely by talking about it, or looking at a filmstrip. For high level learning, questions have to be asked and answers have to be found. The best way to do that is to *interview* people.

INTERVIEW TECHNIQUES WILL BOOST LEARNING

- Interview people? Like reporters on television? Like newspaper men do on the streets?
- Exactly. And these reporters are very good at their jobs.
- We'd like to interview people, too.
- We could interview people in the neighborhood.

See?—Even your littlest children are ready now for your preplanned lesson on interview techniques, which are:

1. To choose a specific person to interview, with parental permission and possibly, some supervision. In this neigh-

borhood unit, the children might choose the baker or the ice cream man, or the doorman in front of an apartment house. They might choose the postman or the policeman, or any one of a dozen workers that appeal to them. After deciding on the interviewee, the thing to do is to make an appointment for an interview.

2. To have a good reason for wanting this interview. A good reason in this instance is to find out about the person's work and about his background.

3. To know how to draw this person out and get him talking. Sometimes, an interviewee might just say *yes* or *no*, so you have to ask good questions. There are six kinds of good questions that almost guarantee good answers:

Four begin with *W*.
One begins with *H*.
One begins with *I*.

And these questions go something like this:

Why are you a baker?
When did you first become interested in baking?
Where were you when the idea of becoming a baker first occurred to you?
What three funny things happened to you in this store?
How would you answer if a customer complained that:

the bread was stale?
the rolls were soggy?
the icing contained a fly?
the change you gave her was wrong?

If you were young again, why would you or wouldn't you go into the same business?

If you had a son, would you advise him to be a baker? Why?

4. To behave in a formal and well-mannered way during the interview. Introduce yourself when you come in. Don't sit down until you're asked to do so. Ask your prepared questions, but don't interrupt the person if he wants to ramble. Be sure to say "Thank you" when the interview is over, and close the door softly behind you when you leave.

Now it's all very well to understand the techniques of interviewing, but putting them into practice is not easy for children. So practice them. Let the class engage in role playing, as a temporary committee of three interviews:

* a child who pretends to be garrulous,
* a child who pretends to be recalcitrant,
* a child who pretends to be hostile,
* a child who is cooperative.

And for homework that night, ask the children to interview their fathers or mothers. Remind them of the characteristics of good questions: the four W's, the one H, the one I.

Follow this up the next day by isolating the difficulties the children encountered at home, together with the ways in which they handled these difficulties.

At this point, no matter what your grade level, all your children will want to be on interviewing committees. Let them. Give them all chances to practice interview techniques! It will take at least a dozen committees to interview the different kinds of people who live and work in your neighborhood.

So implemented, interviewing techniques will net your class three returns:

* They will increasingly involve your children in sharing committee and class responsibilities.
* They will move your social studies program along at a lively pace.

- They will come in mighty useful, when, later in the term, your children engage in making up a newspaper —a simple kind of fact sheet in the lower grades, a more professional news sheet in the upper grades.

BUSINESS LETTER SKILLS WILL EXTEND HORIZONS FOR LEARNING

When the older children planned their saved-day-trip, they manifested readiness for two skills that get things done. These are:

Skill #1—knowing where to obtain general information.
Skill #2—knowing where to obtain specific information.

Since your older children will want to go *far*—at least to the moon—they will need considerable help in working out plans for one practical red-letter day. So help them.

For locating general trip information, have the class bring in newspapers, travel guides, and an assortment of road maps, which are theirs for the asking at the nearby gas stations. Then give them a lesson in scanning these printed materials for the purpose of pinpointing travel possibilities: public parks and landmarks, government buildings and reconstructed villages, ocean liners and airports, churches, mines, publishing houses, baseball training camps and reservoirs.

To find out what specific inducements these possibilities offer, the children will need to write for information. Because they will need to know where to write, call their attention to the almanac and show them how to use it. Here, they will find listings of public organizations, government agencies and general services, together with their addresses.

Now for the actual writing of these letters. You will encounter no resistance from your class when you teach and/ or review the format of a business letter. And your children will buy the idea that a business letter that gets things done is built on the four C's of:

- *Courtesy:* Avoid the worn out "Dear Sir" salutation. It is more courteous to address the person one is writing to by his correct title. (But do the children know who should be addressed as Manager, President, Curator, Director, Your Excellency, The Honorable, the Right Reverend?) Refer again to the almanac and have children look up Forms of Address!

  If your inventory doesn't include almanacs, send your children to the school library. And dust off those old interview techniques and appoint a committee to interview the librarian herself!

- *Conciseness:* To business people, time is money. They have little time or patience for long, rambling letters. Children who write business letters should say what they have to say concisely.

- *Clarity:* It is not wise to write for "full information" because this might result in 50 pages of technical material or a couple of leaflets which are of no interest to children. It is better to ask for specific information, such as:

  What services or exhibits do you offer for school children?
  What days and hours are you open to the public?
  Do you have guided tours?
  Is there an admission charge?
  What is the best route to take from my school to your place?

- *Correctness:* One of the marks of an educated person is his ability to write a neat letter with correct spelling, punctuation, and sentence structure.

What better chance could you possibly devise for practicing proofreading skills than in this very situation, when the

children are writing important business letters? Because these
letters really are important to the children, they will do their
best to observe the 4 C's, and you will see to it that their
best is acceptable by checking every one of the letters before
it goes off in the mail.

Once children have mastered some of these techniques
of learning for their immediate purposes, they are on the
verge of putting these techniques to work for larger purposes,
such as:

- an exhibit to show off their wanderings,
- a newspaper to report their doings,
- a play to demonstrate their resourcefulness.

Working independently, in committee, and under your
guidance they will operate with a common purpose, with
self-formulated rules, and with a drive that harnesses their
enormous proclivities for work. They will operate as a cohesive group, convinced they can do anything and that they
can do it all themselves.

But you will know otherwise, because you know the
threefold secret of the pro:

- You know that the pro operates from the driver's seat
  to release learning power.
- You know she remains in the driver's seat to direct this
  learning power into the kind of achievement the cultural community looks for.
- You know that she perches in the driver's seat with a
  sense of wonder and excitement and anticipation. And
  you know that with a sixth sense, she guides her
  children by remote control.

If knowing this secret leaves you just a little shaken, it
means only that you have glimpsed the glory of your career
but worry about the terrain. You fear you might stumble and
make mistakes. And indeed you might, and you will. You
will need to be concerned, every day of your teaching life,

about *your* techniques and your children's learning. And you would do well to compare your ways with the ways of the best teachers in your school, your district, and your country. So—see your principal and delight him with a request to observe a colleague, and begin with that comparison at once!

3

Developing Imaginative Techniques

for Promoting Reading

So important is the need for literate citizens today, and so widespread is the publicity concerning this need, that *reading* has virtually become a fighting word, tinged with hysteria.

When then, you meet your new "average" class, your first concern is with their reading level. You study their record cards and test scores. You administer informal book tests. You review your instructional materials. But whether your class checks out on grade or not, two things are certain:

1. You are sure to find a wide reading range, within the group, that has been increasing about two or three years, for every year the class has spent in school. If you have a second grade, some children may still be non-readers, while others will be handling third and fourth grade library books. If you have a sixth grade, don't be surprised to find some children reading on grade three level, and others zooming ahead on 10th and 12th year materials.

2. You are also sure to find, if you probe deeper, that almost every child has moved through the grades with some specific blind spots in mechanics and in comprehension,

and that these are noted over and over again on his reading card. There's a repetitiveness about these notations which indicates that these spotty difficulties generally do not go away.

Try another approach

This does not have to happen in your room! And it won't if you begin by acquainting your children with their most recent standard reading scores. (Should you have no recent scores, see your principal immediately, and ask for permission to administer such a test.) Then surprise your children by dramatizing the reading levels in your room. Draw two staircases on your chalkboard, and, if yours is, for example, a

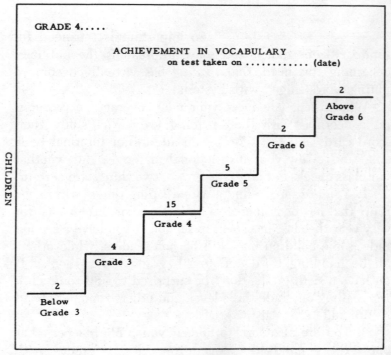

Figure 4A

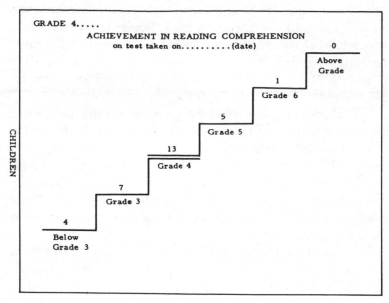

Figure 4B

fourth grade, your staircases may look like those depicted in Figures 4A and 4B.

Immediately, your children will become aware of the fact that standard reading tests check out two different areas: of meaning of words when they are by themselves; and the meaning of words when they are strung together into sentences and paragraphs. They will also notice, if your class runs true to form, that more children do better on vocabulary tests than on comprehension tests.

So much for the class picture which is valuable because it indicates group gradations in achievement. But reading is a personal affair with personal drives and difficulties. So tell each child his own reading scores, but do so privately to avoid possible embarrassment and humiliation. And that night, for homework, devise very personal assignments. Ask each child to bring in a personal list of reading difficulties that he would like you to help him with. Don't be astonished if the list ranges from such items as: "I can't sound out words," "I stumble over long words," "Sometimes I can't pronounce words with *ough* or *oe*, or *ie*," to "I leave off the endings of my words," "When a sentence is long, I forget what it's about," "I can read the words but the questions mix me up!"

Children are more frequently aware of their shortcomings than we realize. They don't overcome these shortcomings because they don't know how to, although they want desperately to succeed. So involve them in a Success Story! Put them on their mettle. Get them to verbalize their difficulties under your direction, and then help them! Help them to help themselves with suitable materials and compassionate teacher guidance.

Without ever forgetting these lists of personal difficulties, take the heat off the *mechanics* of reading, and emphasize first, last and always, the broad picture of reading—what it is, and what it's all about.

TALK WITH YOUR CHILDREN AND LISTEN!

Listen with a sensitive ear as they consider such questions as:

What, actually is reading? Is it a subject? Is it a language? Suppose all the reading materials in the school disappeared, would that mean you couldn't learn how to read? Would you then miss out on your education? If you had your way, would you read more or less? Would you read all the time? Would you stop reading? Why?

If you were the teacher, and this class read the way the "staircases" indicate, would you teach the children more reading? Would you let some stop altogether? What would you have the children read, and how would you get them to do it?

Your children will soon see for themselves that reading is not a subject like social studies or arithmetic. They will also agree that nobody just reads reading! Anybody who reads, reads something: letters, ads, recipes, directions, newspapers. Instead of being a subject, reading turns out to be a tool that is used for various purposes. When your children read comic books, it's for fun. When they read assignments, it's for work. When they read library books, it's for pleasure.

These are excellent reasons for reading, but you have deeper reasons. So this might be a good time to acquaint your children with a basic fact of life: that *you* are charged with the development of literate citizens, and that *they* are in school for exactly the same reason—to become literate citizens!

Would your children consider themselves sufficiently literate? If they check the dictionary, they'll discover that a literate person is one who is well read. And a well read person is one who not only reads more, but who also gets more out of his reading!

But what *is* reading? Your children, being realists, will say that:

- Reading is recognizing the letters of the alphabet.
- Reading is sounding out and recognizing whole words.
- Reading is recognizing printed words that are put together in sentences, and then making sense out of the sentences.

You could almost stop at this definition of reading when you think of the countless children who've taught themselves to read because they wanted to, and of your immigrant forebears who learned the alphabet, sounded out the words, recognized them in sentences, and became highly successful citizens.

But you don't stop, because this definition is mainly a definition of reading mechanics. And, although reading mechanics and phonics are indeed very important, they are not a part of reading, as such. They are, rather, skills that should be considered in skill building periods, altogether *apart* from your reading periods. So you push for the deeper definition of reading-as-communication.

To your children, reading is already a form of communication, when they bother to read on their own. Then it's to get the message: the graffiti on the school wall, the strike placards in the street, a friend's secret code book, sister's diary, big brother's sex manual. On their own, they do not read just for the sake of reading! And when you assign a printed selection, they read to find out what the author is saying behind those printed symbols: perhaps he's telling 100 jokes; perhaps he's giving directions for making kites or model planes or candy; perhaps he's describing a boy's feelings when his home is being torn down.

Involve your children in planning for literate citizenship

If you look at reading experiences as communication experiences, then your aim will be to develop a reading program that challenges your children so strongly that they will find it worthwhile to invest their time, their minds, and their limitless zeal in learning to read beyond the level of word calling, on to the level of literate citizenship.

But there are conditions that have to be met.

Some Prerequisites to Getting Your Reading Program Off the Ground

Here are a few of the things you will have to see to:

- You will have to provide your children with the ways and means of using a multiplicity of real-life reading materials in addition to the reading texts in your room.
- You will have to provide guidance in, and mastery of half a dozen reading skills that will enable your children to extract the message that the author is trying to communicate.
- You will have to sharpen your children's insights so

they will get more than is actually being said on the printed page.

But first, a word of caution plus two *do*'s and *don't*'s:

The word of caution concerns the reading materials you find in your room. The best your school provides frequently is not reason enough, as far as your children are concerned, for learning to read better. This doesn't mean you won't be able to lift the general reading level of your class. Of course you can do that with the proper teaching skills and with carefully selected basal readers. But for *significant* reading this isn't enough!

Do use, in addition to the reading materials already in your room, varied and unorthodox materials with your children. Everything is grist for the reading mill, from experience charts to throwaways, community releases, industrial bulletins, newspapers, paperbacks and library books. Involve your children in reading widely, and bear down on reading as a tool for the purpose of getting the message from the math, social studies and science texts.

Do use materials that will further your own expertise in teaching. Dip into all the reading manuals you can lay your hands on. Search for ideas and approaches that will help you develop particular reading skills. Try for the long view, meaning the long range sequence of graded skills.

Don't embrace a basal reading series to the exclusion of other reading materials. Your children need greater breadth and greater exposure.

It's true that the newer reading series are excellent and oriented to today. Each lesson is expertly planned. Each new skill fits into a sequence. Each new word is methodically repeated in the subsequent pages to ensure reenforcement and retention.

And yet *the national index of reading retardation is climbing steadily*. Some authorities believe that this is due to the fact that too many teachers limit too many children to the one or two basal readers in the room. And in so doing, they automatically limit their children to a controlled number of pages per day, a controlled number of communication experiences, and a controlled vocabulary.

Consider the stranglehold of the controlled vocabulary if you don't plan a reading program that includes rich and varied reading experiences. Experts estimate that average English-speaking children have a listening vocabulary that ranges from 18,000 to 23,000 words at age six. And this is not surprising because: the young TV listeners are familiar with words that were totally unknown or rarely used, 50 years ago; and listening, they casually acquire whole space vocabularies and armament vocabularies. They acquire weather and gourmet and political campaign vocabularies.

Yet these same children, when limited to a basal reading series or even two, leave Grade 6 with a reading vocabulary of 3,000 to 6,000 words! They have literally been kept from seeing in print the thousands of words that they had in their listening vocabularies when they first came to school in Grade 1.

Don't discard your basal reader in your zeal to extend your children's reading. Used judiciously, it will serve you well. Watch and learn when you conduct a lesson from the reader. Make note of the prepared plans in the manual. Look for and adapt the techniques of planning that carry a lesson to completion: the format, the organization, the questions, the nailed-down summary. Observe the planned step by step development of any one reading skill. And note that while you're struggling to build a reading program that is solid and dynamic, you'll find a basal reader in your hand, · a sustaining and supportive prop.

Two Plans Necessary for Developing Literate Citizens

With the *Do*'s and *Don't*'s out of the way, you are ready to look to your overall reading program, based on your children's desire to read and your desire to develop literate citizens.

And immediately, you see the need for two separate plans: because a literate citizen is one who *appreciates literature*, you will be planning a strong program in literature, and because a literate citizen is one who *practices citizenship* with understanding and critical analysis, you will be planning a strong program in critical or creative reading.

Plan #1—To Develop Literate Citizens Who Appreciate Literature

Once children have progressed beyond the bare rudiments of phonics and word recognition, they are ready to read literature on their own. If your children are advanced readers, they'll be wanting advanced books. If they are reluctant, hesitant, halting or barely beginning readers, no matter. There are high interest books on every reading level. Your job is to make them available to your children.

Immerse your children in personal reading, and here's how to do it; First scout the children's room of the local public library. Introduce yourself to the librarian. Tell her about your children, your projects and your plans. Pick up a dozen application slips just in case some of your children have never yet joined the library. You'll infect your children with your own enthusiasm when you tell them about your talk with the librarian, about the coming Children's Story Hour, and about the magazine and recordings, books and picture collections that are available. All free. All there for the borrowing! Your class will promptly want to go to the library, too.

As you plan this trip, open up to your children the kinds of books that are available. And you do this in terms of their interests, personalities, local mores, and needs.

Use your chalkboard. Even reluctant readers will glow when recognized:

- Tom likes horses? Splendid!
- Matthew? Why, heroes and presidents and astronauts, of course!
- Jacqueline? Fairy tales.
- Terry? Cowboys!
- Bobby? Lost mines, secret caverns and treasure maps!
- Rich? Science books.
- Janice? Fantasy.
- Alvin? Science fiction!
- And Paul likes mysteries, while Mary likes books that tell how to make doll clothes!

By the time you've listed the preferences of each of your children, you'll find that the whole spectrum of books has been included on your chalkboard. Take your children one step farther. Teach them that books in a library are arranged according to categories: animal stories in one place; fairy tales and fantasy in another; adventure stories, here; mysteries there; and whole sets of shelves in another area, reserved entirely for biographies, science and how-to books.

Have the class secretary copy the list of preferences for you, and then, as you review the treats waiting at the library, suggest to the children that they show, by proper behavior, their respect for the books in the Children's Room.

And, when you arrive at the library, direct your children to the shelves that you know they are interested in.

Nothing, however, will turn your children off and away from wide and happy reading as much as a disappointing trip to the library. It's very frustrating to be unable to find something special, or to be rushed and told to hurry up. So permit plenty of time for browsing when you get there. And it would be a good idea to review, before starting on this trip, ways of previewing a book to see if it appeals.

Planned this way, a trip to the library will fire your children's interests. Keep that fire going. Whether your chil-

dren are first graders or sixth, they will require your un-
flagging and supportive enthusiasm. This you can give them
through periodic book-sharing talks in class. Get into the
act yourself. Pick up a good book you like and say, casually,
"I just happened to reread this book, and I find that . . ."
or, "I came across this brand new book in the library, and do
you know that. . . ." In this way you give the first book
talk, and your children will need very little nudging to fall
into line and do likewise.

Now immerse your children in a group reading project.
The habit of omniverous and diversified reading is one of the
greatest gifts you can give your children. And you can give
them more than that if you involve them in directed group
experiences so that they read widely and appreciatively,
around a pivotal theme, and share their reading.

Any theme will do.

With very young children, who, for example, may be
studying weather, you will want to open up the world of
poetry about rainy days and snowy days, stormy days and
windy days. Your job then, is to read extensively to the class.
Your children will also have a job: to compile illustrated
booklets filled with rexographed copies of these exciting
poems you've read to them; to try their collective hands at
writing class poetry in the same vein; and to select the best
for the class library table.

With upper grade children, who've just completed a
unit on Early America, you might want to consider the feelings of those early pioneers as they settled the land. They
had little time, less patience, and a good measure of contempt
for the vanities of society. Your aim? To guide your children
to find out for themselves what motives, what feelings, what
drives propelled those people across the wilderness. What
was it they cheered about, grieved about, admired, feared
and condemned? What was it they prized and believed in
with a conviction stronger than death? And what better way

to communicate the texture of those times than by way of the energy, bounce and simplicity of the nineteenth century poets!

Three steps will launch your children on such a literary venture:

* Step 1 starts before ever a single page of a single poem is read.
* Step 2 continues with the reading of the page.
* Step 3 follows through, beyond the page.

For Step 1—reading-before-the-page, you will have to make yourself warmly familiar with several good anthologies. You will need to know, in order to guide your children, that the voices speaking for those times were the voices of John Greenleaf Whittier and Clement Moore, Edgar Allen Poe and Henry Wadsworth Longfellow, Walt Whitman, Oliver Wendell Holmes, Charles L. Reason, Paul Laurence Dunbar, and scores of others—some white, some black and some anonymous.

And then you will want to communicate to your children your admiration and respect for these voices, so you will begin by reading excerpts to them. Read sincerely and with feeling and with whatever histrionic ability you may possess. But don't overdo it and don't beat a poem to death with too much discussion. Appreciation is a fragile thing. Let your children react as they can.

Read your excerpts and watch.

Some children will respond more readily than others to the tug and pull of poems that communicate the freshness of country living: "Snowbound," "The Barefoot Boy," "The Night Before Christmas." Some will be entranced by "The Bells," because fear of the unknown is a universal feeling. Some will be moved deeply by the simplicity and grandeur of "Hiawatha's Childhood," others, by the hurrying hoofbeats of Paul Revere's steed because "the fate of a nation was riding that night."

Watch as you read the poem titled "Life," written by the famous Negro poet, Dunbar, about "A crust of bread/ A corner to sleep in/ A minute to smile/ And an hour to weep in."

Watch as you introduce the motivating theme of the time that "Life is real! Life is earnest!"; the bolstering belief that "Mine eyes have seen the glory of the coming of the Lord"; the patriotic awareness of the new flag, capsuled in "Hats off!/ Along the street there comes,/ A blare of bugles, a ruffle of drums," and then "Blue and crimson and white it shines."

All this you do with your children before you ask them to read a single page of a single poem!

Now, Step 2—the-reading-of-the-page, will be a meaningful possibility for your children. And so you send them to the anthologies, the book shelves and the library to look for poems that appeal especially to them, and that say something special about the people of Early America. You ask them to return with favorites to share with the class. To avoid the interminable reading aloud of lengthy poems, invite the children to read "appetizers," meaning bits and pieces, exciting phrases, rollicking rhythms, contagious rhymes.

Your children will do more than read just a single page of poetry because they'll have to read many poems and many poets before settling on a favorite. They will read infinitely more than your most carefully directed homework assignments could have induced them to read. And when they share their favorites—jingles, limericks, sonnets and epic poems—literary tastes will be shaped as they should be, through comparison and not through directive.

But Step 3—the-reading-beyond-the-page, will come through as proof positive if the nineteenth century poets are really communicating with your children. Then you will see a poetry corner appearing in your room; and busts and pictures of poets, a display of dioramas, a frieze of word pictures, a growing collection of pupil-made anthologies and a bulletin board of exciting quotations under such provocative captions as WHO SAID THIS? WHEN? WHERE? AND WHY?

Your class may even decide to select a class poet, perhaps Longfellow, who is a great favorite with children. If they do, don't be surprised if they post his picture and display his works and any pertinent artifacts they can borrow at the local museum. And then they may just naturally get a placard, letter it with the words WAYSIDE INN, tack it on your door, and turn your room into a Poetry Center, complete with a pupil-made fireplace for sitting around, in order to read "Evangeline" and other poems by Longfellow.

Now let your children show off their enthusiasm for Early American poetry. Let them prepare a program that spills over into the assembly. Without cracking the whip for prescribed memorization, you can guide them through a choral speaking program that will stay with them for life.

In the same way, you can conduct your children through the reading of hundreds of tales and anecdotes, biographies, speeches and stories that illuminate the history of our country. But make sure that you alert the librarian so that she will have on hand not only a limitless supply of books, but also a collection of filmstrips and recordings of prose selections. Such audio visuals are a very special must for those of your children who are still poor readers, but who should not be deprived of the chance to become acquainted with the literary giants of the times.

These wonderful things do not just happen in any old classroom. They can be made to happen in your room by your unquenchable enthusiasm and your unshakable belief that children will read and read omnivorously, when it's worth their while to read. And when you have brought them to this point, you will know that you are beginning to achieve your first aim—to develop literate citizens who appreciate literature!

Plan #2—To Develop Literate Citizens Who Practice Citizenship

Your aim being twofold, you now turn your attention to developing literate citizens with the emphasis on citizenship. This means developing thinking citizens who can appraise our culture by way of critical reading.

To develop such a program of critical reading, you and your children need to be very clear about the fact: that there are three levels of reading comprehension: reading the line; reading between the lines; and reading beyond the lines—that there are specific reading skills which can be applied, level by level, to unlock the knowledge, the thinking and the power that is stored in the printed lines.

Three levels will carry your children through to critical reading

Reading on Level 1 means reading-the-lines. When children are asked to find simple ideas and details on a printed page, they are being asked to read only the lines of print, and to answer such simple questions as: Who helped pitch the tent? Why was he in the forest? What did his friends do? How did his dog help him? How did he manage to catch the fish after he lost his pole?

This is reading for simple, low level comprehension. It is an important skill, but too many children spend too many years answering questions of this sort. That's because of the overwhelming availability of attractive and carefully prepared exercises: workbooks, test sheets and programmed materials, all equipped with instant answers for the teacher's use.

Such exercises will not fire your children with the desire to read half a dozen books about camping or fishing, neither will they challenge them to read critically. Your children deserve better than that. So—move them on to Level 2.

Reading on Level 2 means reading-between-the-lines. To read between the lines, your children need to read thoughtfully. This means they must learn to read different selections in different ways:

- They will read literature with a listening ear, for tone and mood, dialogue and emotional involvement.
- They will read science reports with a sharp eye, searching for cause and effect.
- They will read math material with the problem in mind, noting details carefully.
- They will read social studies texts with an awareness of the big picture, searching for big ideas, space-time sequences, and relationships between people and places.
- They will read newspaper accounts and editorials with a cautious attitude, looking for evidence of bias and slant.

This is not to say that your children must mull over every word in order to become critical readers. If they are reading chemical formulas, cooking recipes, or poetry, then mulling is in order. If they are hunting for numbers in the telephone book, then mulling is out and speed is in.

By themselves, neither mulling nor speed will turn your children into thoughtful readers. For that, they need the proper reading skills. So here are three skills and three techniques that older children will find indispensable and younger children will be able to grow on. Some of these are rapid reading skills, some are work study skills, and some are detecting techniques invaluable for critical reading of newspapers, propaganda and ads.

Reading Skills to Pierce the Comprehension Curtain!

Skimming is a rapid reading skill that is useful for breezing through new material, and the aim is crystal clear:

What's all this about? What's in it for me? Is it worth reading thoroughly?

To skim efficiently, your children need to be on the lookout for six signposts: the introductory paragraph, the captions and subcaptions, the first and last sentences of paragraphs, the key words that point out the framework of the selection (the *who, what, when, where, why* and *how*), the clues that propel the reader through the content (*nevertheless, therefore, in this way, in spite of, in addition, but, because*), the summary paragraph.

Scanning is another rapid reading skill that is useful in tracking down specifically wanted facts: names, dates, statistics, special words and phrases. Children find scanning a handy skill when they need to locate certain details for building a time or distance sequence; or for developing tables for purposes of comparison.

For such checking out of specifics, almost any printed material may be scanned: textbooks and dictionaries, encyclopedias, road maps, time tables, indexes, market listings and newspapers.

Outlining is a multiple organizing skill that is useful for extracting ideas and facts from the contents. Your children will have no trouble learning how to write an outline, if you develop it this way:

Start with a modified outline. If, for example, your children are reading about mammals in the jungle, work it up as suggested in Figure 5.

Name of Mammal	Size	Kind of Fur	Food	Food Gathering Equipment	Fighting Equipment

Figure 5

Move on to the heading outline. A look at most printed selections (especially chapters in textbooks) will show the material arranged under main headings in bold print, and under secondary headings in lighter print. Have your children read, discuss and copy these headings, and they will have made up their first simple outline—clear and to the point!

Follow this with the development of the main idea outline. First, have your children scrutinize each of the paragraphs for the *main idea*. Alert them to the fact that the main idea may appear either at the beginning or at the end of the paragraph. If it appears at the beginning, then it is supported in the subsequent sentences with pertinent details, and the paragraph has been structured like this:

Main Idea

detail

detail

detail

If, however, the main idea appears at the end of the paragraph, then this main idea has been developed by a mass of preceding details, and the paragraph has been structured like this:

detail

detail

detail

Main Idea

With a little practice, your children will be able to select and to separate the main ideas from the multitudinous
details in any paragraph—but use caution! Make certain to
keep the vocabulary simple when you are developing a skill.
Learning will take place much more rapidly and effectively,
if you work on one difficulty at a time.

Follow through with the sentence outline, then with the
phrase outline, and then you are only a lesson away from
the word outline.

And another word of caution. Although it's not difficult
to learn how to outline, it's very easy to forget, so provide
periodic reenforcement. Vary your approach. Use social
studies and science and newspaper materials. And, when
necessary, return your children to their English textbooks
for precision in outlining.

Detecting Techniques Will Spot Implications!

Alert your children to the implications lurking between
the lines of print in emotionally colored language. Show
them how to scrutinize words for emotional impact. Equip
them with techniques for spotlighting slant and bias. Turn
them loose on newspapers, magazines, texts, reference materials and trade publications. And sharpen their critical
reading abilities:

- By showing them how to look for the *transfer of emotions* that takes place in a sentence because of such
  words as "The *gallant* captain seized the *flag* and
  raced across the lines to his *mother*." Now, this captain might be a traitor. He might be a deserter. He
  might be a collaborator. Before you can read further,
  however, you're all for him because of three emotionally packed words: *gallant, flag,* and *mother*.
- By showing them how to detect the sway of *good
  names* and *bad names* in such statements as "The
  presidential candidate is a dynamo of *energy*, a colos-

sus of *understanding,* a reservoir of help to the *poor.*"
Now note the bad names with which his enemies describe him: "The presidential candidate is a *pusher,*
a *pretender* to intelligence, a *diverter* of funds to the
public whim!"

- By showing them how to perceive *card stacking*
which is a way of emphasizing good qualities and
omitting all others. Check TV commercials and magazine ads for examples of card stacking, such as. . . .
Buy TONI Toothpaste. It tastes *better.* It lasts *longer.*
It costs *less.* It makes your teeth *whiter!* . . . Your
perceptive children will ask, "Better and longer and
whiter than *what?*"

In your drive to develop literate citizens, you've em-
powered your children to read the lines and to read between
the lines. They've learned how to abstract ideas and facts
and to organize them in an outline. But your quest is not yet
over—not until you've provided time and opportunity for
pupil *reaction,* and this brings you to planning for Level 3.

Reading on Level 3 means reading-beyond-the-lines. If
your children are now reading intelligently and critically,
their reactions to given selections will be evidenced in ways
that point to practicing citizenship: they will be reading
more extensively because they will be acquiring new interests; they will be behaving more constructively because their
reading will modify their understanding, and they will react
accordingly.

Suppose you've just completed a Health Unit about
proper indoor and outdoor clothing. You've noticed considerable interest in the borrowing of trade books in this area.
You've been deluged with posters, dioramas and reports.
Great! Health learning has taken place! But, is it being practiced? Check your children's footgear on a rainy midmorn-
ing. If Mary Jane is still wearing her storm boots, she's more
than forgetful. She is not reacting constructively. She's not
reading-beyond-the-lines!

In the same way, you can look for reactions to reading in the social studies, in terms of modified behavior. Do your children lean increasingly toward community involvement? Do they participate in clean-up drives? Do they photograph places that need improvement, places that are beautiful, places that serve them? Do they, in turn, help take care of public parks, observe traffic rules, cooperate with trades people? Do they, in your Current Events periods, detect bias and slant, emotionally toned words and stacked cards, *and* do they do something about it? Do they write to the editor? Do they interview government officials, in order to get and to set the record straight?

When you see such growing evidences of reading-beyond-the-lines, you can justifiably feel that you have done a good job in developing literate citizens. But are you sure?

To be sure, you will have to test. It often happens, however, that children engaged in the most scintillating programs show up badly on formal tests, in competition with children engaged in the dullest kinds of programs. Avoid such a catastrophic showing which is fair neither to you, your children, nor your program, and which may bring down upon your head the wrath of your principal and the Local School Board.

You can give your children the chance to shine on formal tests as they deserve to, and you can do it in two ways that are tried and true: by powering them with effective techniques for promoting a self-propelling vocabulary, and by equipping them with test-taking and test-making techniques.

And, if you'll turn to Chapter 4 and to Chapter 11, you'll find these techniques discussed in some detail.

4

Capitalizing on the Children's
Desire to Communicate

The desire to communicate is evidenced in the first strangled cry at birth, and increases through the babbling and chattering stages of early childhood. Yet, when children come to school, differences are sharp. Some communicate with considerable eloquence, some speak with their guards up, some are withdrawn and almost mute.

Teacher 1—My children communicate all the time. They'd talk all day if I let them.

Teacher 2—Mine would write notes constantly if I didn't put my foot down.

The ability to communicate depends on the *me* concept

This is the general impression . . . that children talk incessantly, but it just isn't so. Only children who relate well with others are able to communicate easily. Such children have a strong *ME* concept, and are able to project their thoughts and feelings outward. Those who cannot communicate easily are the inhibited ones. These need an accepting classroom environment to offset negative influences and to boost that negative self-image. In an accepting environment, those who are unduly shy will develop competence for expressing themselves in writing. Those who reach out naturally, will reach farther orally, and in written communication.

Whatever their degree of language competence, when they come to school they need newer and larger skills because now they are members of constantly changing groups. And, to be effective group members, they need new language learnings in a hurry.

FOUR NEW LANGUAGE SKILLS ARE NEEDED IN SCHOOL

They need to know how to share in-school and out-of-school happenings with each other, in ways that are suited to the listening and reading abilities of their peers—without rambling, without endless repetitions, and without fantastic incoherence.

They need to know how to participate successfully in class activities involving planning, organizing, comparing, reporting and evaluating.

They need to know how to project their feelings by way of language instead of kicks, slaps, punches and howls.

They need to know how to express ideas by way of precise and colorful language.

Teacher 3—I say, "Surround the children with an attractive room and a stimulating class environment, and they'll have plenty to express, verbally and in writing."

Teacher 4—Your environment may be stimulating, but that doesn't mean your children will automatically express themselves with increased facility.

Teacher 5—If it's skill development you're after, get a good set of English workbooks, put your children through the exercises, and hope for the best.

Teacher 6—I know a better way. I put *myself* through

the English workbooks. This way I get to understand the sequential development of any particular skill. Then I use the functional approach with my children, and it works!

VARIED APPROACHES LEAD
TO VARIED LANGUAGE LEARNINGS

And here you have the standard approaches to language development in the schools:

- There's the stimulating environment approach, which should certainly exist in your room but which of and by itself, motivates children to talk or write in the same slight degree that beautiful seascapes or ravishing sunsets motivate adults to take pen in hand.
- There's the workbook approach with its prepackaged developmental step-by-step instruction in the structure of skills—and the commonplace of children consistently scoring high in workbook learning but failing to apply this learning to oral or written expression.
- And there's the functional approach, meaning that important activities are discussed and written up for real reasons. It's in functional communication that children call for skills and techniques years before the course of study calls for them.

THE FUNCTIONAL APPROACH PROVIDES TWO AVENUES
FOR WRITTEN COMMUNICATION

There are two kinds of functional language activities: the practical and the personal.

Practical writing is used in practical classroom situations: to draw up plans for routines and for special occasions; to reproduce the happenings on a trip; to say "Thank you" to another class for an assembly program; to describe an interview, take notes, write up a précis, a book review, or a letter asking for information.

Children engage in this kind of writing readily, and as readily accept your emphasis on learning the mechanics of spelling, punctuation, penmanship and neatness.

Personal writing is used to express assorted feelings: of personal drives such as hope and fear, anger and joy, sorrow and desire; and of personal reactions, by way of the five senses, to experiences in or out of school.

Such writing is often imaginative, colorful, highly creative and delightfully unsophisticated because it is so personal. Your children will want to take off with little regard for the mechanics they have learned so painstakingly in their practical writing experiences. Let them. Place emphasis where it belongs in personal writing—on the expression of thoughts and feelings. Say nothing about a messy paper, on the first reading. If it's really illegible, ask the author to read it to you. Give praise where praise is due, for an idea or a well turned phrase. If it's good enough, he'll take great pains to rewrite it properly. If it isn't good enough, why make him waste time rewriting it?

How to Foster Functional Writing in the Lower Grades

Combine practical and personal writing! And here's how to do it. Suppose your class had just listened to a guidance program on the radio. The topic? Should seven-year-old children get an allowance? The discussion that follows is lively. The agreement, naturally, unanimous.

Shall we write this up?

Of course!

And so you write up an experience chart that the children dictate, complete with quotations, question marks and exclamation points.

If you stop here, your little children will have experienced a cooperative writing activity that is basically practical. But you can make it a personal and highly individual writing experience for them. Suggest they consider and write up their own experiences with parents: Bedtime hours? Slammed doors? Routine baths? Scrubbed hands? Brushed teeth? What else? Your children will view their problems with enthusiastic good humor and be ready to gallop away on long, involved and endless accounts of "How You Cannot Win in My House."

Caution #1—Little children have little attention spans, so keep them to little writing projects, or they will never finish, become frustrated, and soon turn away from all writing experiences. Avoid such a state of affairs by challenging them to brevity. Can they write a pithy four-line dialogue with nothing important left out, telling how:

- My mother insists, "................"
- I ask, "........................?"
- She says, "......................"
- And I answer, "...................."

In this way, you get personal involvement by the children, plus a practice session in the use of quotation marks!

Caution #2—Some children may not yet be capable of writing individual compositions. That's to be expected, so have those few copy the cooperative experience chart from the board and then illustrate it in terms of their own home situations.

Follow this combination of practical and personal writing whenever you can, because it gives you a chance to develop a variety of language skills through a naturally developing series of writing activities. And it provides opportunities for your children to communicate on a variety of levels.

Use the here and now to take off on a series of lessons in communication. Is the day bright and sunny? Gray and windy? Look out the window and see! Windy? Splendid! Ask the children to tell what the wind did, as they were coming to school!

- The wind whistled in my ears and dried up my mouth.
- The wind snatched off my hat and slapped it across my face.
- The wind smelled like fried eggs and bacon.
- The wind blew smoke from a man's pipe.
- The wind turned me round and round and pushed me!

So much for what the wind did. Can anyone think of some words that describe the wind? *And you move into a lesson on vocabulary development!* Your list on the chalkboard will soon include such words as: *fresh, damp, gusty, noisy, breezy, gentle, soft,* and maybe even *blustery!*

Don't let this activity fade out now that the children are expressing their feelings about the wind in sentences and in descriptive words. Show them how other people feel about the wind. Read from two or three selected poems about winds, and encourage them to listen for good lines, exciting lines, and special lines and words they like the best. And list these on your board too. Then reread the favorite poem, and since the class has had little experience in writing original poetry, show them how they, too, can make up poems! And you start with the simplest rhymes.

To make up simple rhymes about the wind, ask the children to help you make up two lists of words: one, to list the names of the different kinds of winds; the other, to list words that tell what these winds do. And you will, of course, press into service the picture dictionaries and the elementary dictionaries that are in your room, as well as your own copy of a children's thesaurus. When the lists are ready, get the words onto cards. Then put the cards that name the winds, down the left side of your flannel board. After that, ask the children to find the cards that tell what the winds do, and match them, in a second column down your flannel board, and your board will look something like this:

Column 1	Column 2
Winds	blow
Breezes	snatch
Zephyrs	puff
Gales	roar
Gusts	slap
Storms	howl
Tornadoes	whirl

Only two more steps and your children will have composed rhymes! So in the third column on your flannel board, you write alternately the words GIRLS and BOYS, and then, working on one line at a time, you ask for words that tell what boys and girls do, but what they do must rhyme with the word in Column 2! And soon, after a score of hilarious contributions, the rhymes on your board may look something like this:

Column 1	Column 2	Column 3	Column 4
Winds	blow	girls	grow
Breezes	snatch	boys	catch
Zephyrs	puff	girls	huff
Gales	roar	boys	snore
Gusts	slap	girls	nap
Storms	howl	boys	growl
Tornadoes	whirl	girls	twirl

Fun? Of course! Your children will be delighted with their new-found rhyming ability and will want to do more of the same, for homework. So here's an assignment to be done with dictionaries in hand. Since little children are always reading and talking about animals, ask them to fold their homework paper in four vertical columns, and then to proceed as follows: list ten animals they particularly like in Column 1; list ten words in Column 2 that tell how these animals move; list ten things they see in the kitchen in

Column 3; and list ten words in Column 4 that go with the words in Column 3, and rhyme with the words in Column 2. And you may be getting rhymes like:

Column 1	Column 2	Column 3	Column 4
Robins	hop	mothers	shop.
Snakes	glide	icecubes	slide.
Cats	stalk	children	talk.
Ants	scurry	fathers	worry.

So far, your children have been writing only rhymes. They have a long way to go before they're actually writing poetry. Don't rush them. But do move them into a lesson on rhythm. Reread a favorite poem with a good beat. Have the children clap out the beat. Then start them on writing cooperative couplets. Help them by supplying the first line in the form of a question that almost answers itself, e.g.:

Q—What creature likes to swim and swish?
A—A creature that's a great big fish!

Splendid! Write it on the board. Have the children read it aloud and beat out the rhythm. And then, ask another question!

Q—What creatures buzz among the trees?
A—The creatures that are honey bees!

Of course, little children will need more practice of this kind, so develop personal couplets with them every day. By the end of the week, most of them should be able to develop couplets of their own. And they will, if you challenge them and praise them lavishly.

Q—Who has a buckle on her shoe?
A—A little girl named Mary Lou.

Q—And who's got hair cut neat and trim?
A—An eight-year-old, whose name is Tim!

Continue reading lots of poetry to them, but don't make

a fetish of rhyming. A touch of artificiality tends to creep into the writing of children when they force their thoughts to rhyme. So provide just enough of this kind of activity to keep interest in words and expressions high, and be open to exciting topics that your children seem eager to write about. But remember that children like to write about topics that permit them to get into the act.

To get your children into the act in writing you need to involve them in the telling of personal experiences that are grounded in reality. Here are a couple of experiences that are truly real or real with tongue in cheek, and they could happen to any child, at any age:

Topic 1: *I Looked Out My Window*
Topic 2: *My First . . .*

Of and by themselves, topics that you may write on the board are just so many words, and if that is all that you as a teacher do, then the written compositions will also be just so many words. Needed, along with a good topic, is some good developmental discussion guided to give movement and sequence to the writing, and about three writing periods extending over three days to complete the activity.

Suppose then, you start with the topic, "I Looked Out of My Window." Write the topic on the board and ask your children these questions:

What did you see when you looked out the window? (And the discussion will sparkle because your children will have seen anything they wished—elephants, dinosaurs, spacemen, a fish that walked, a music box, a bully, a piece of string, a wood chuck or the captain of the football team, or nothing at all! What did it look like, sound like and do? How did you feel then? What did you do? Then what happened?

On the first day, encourage plenty of discussion and write down the exciting and pertinent words the children use during this discussion. On the second day, review the discussion briefly in terms of the five questions on the board. Remember the short attention span and the need for brevity as you set your children to writing, and hold them, if you can, to half a page. On the third day, glance through the compositions and select the most ingenious to read to the class. Some will have been written by your star pupils, others by your diffident, retiring children, some by your slow children. Don't be surprised. When you develop a good lesson in expression, you are drawing on what's inside! So you read, and, watching the rapt faces of your audience, you know that your young authors are communicating.

Now you come to the correction of the papers, and here, because personal and creative writing is a fragile thing, you encounter two strong opinions: There are those who hold that every error must be noted, corrected and rewritten; and there are those who hold that it's the communication of ideas that is important, and away with the deadly and destructive corrections.

Actually, a middle ground is needed here. When your children engage in *practical* writing, the mechanics must be accurate, and every paper must be carefully corrected and rewritten. When, however, your children engage in personal and creative writing, look at the first draft, primarily for ideas and for the communication of ideas. If there are incoherencies, ask the child to say what he means in another way, so that you may understand it more clearly. Then, ask him to proofread his paper with you, and correct it together with you, so that his writing will really say what he wants it to say. Appreciate his colorful expressions and then—if he knows his paper might be included in the Class Book for the Library Table, you won't have to ask him to rewrite it perfectly. He'll want it perfect, himself!

In developing the second topic, "My First . . ." you follow the same procedure. List the "firsts" that your children propose: the first haircut, the first day at school, the first puppy, the first spanking, the first lie, the first report card, the first party, and dozens of others. Again, you develop a board outline in the form of guiding questions:

1. What most important "first" do you remember?
2. Why do you remember it?
3. How did you feel when it happened?
4. What did you do then?

And again, you guide the topic through to the exciting end, laced with bubbling good humor and shared, of course, with the class.

Next to talking about themselves, children like to write about themselves. This personal pleasure, however, often dims as the years go by. That's because children fail to develop a crackling vocabulary and functional writing skills to match, both of which are predicated on a love of language.

Two Ways to Foster a Love of Language

No matter what the writing activity and what the degree of writing excellence, your children can express their ideas with more zip, excitement, facility and skill. Show them how, by showing them the power of words and the control that sentences can have over these words. And here's how to do that:

Power their vocabulary in two ways: by building familiarity with new words-in-categories; and by developing new word concepts. Prepare and develop charts of words as occasions arise, and you will be including holiday and weather words, social studies and party words, and words about toys and games and trips and feasts, as well as all sorts of unusual words that come up daily in the ordinary course of events . . . List the 300 words that children most frequently use in their writing. Check your manuals for lists of words, include words that are indigenous to your neighborhood groups, and direct your children to listen to intriguing words when you read to them. In this way, you'll be building sensitivity to words, and your children's ideas will be flowing more readily because they'll have this vast store of useful and familiar words to think with!

Caution: It will not do anybody any good, however, if your vocabulary lists grow longer without your children's understanding growing correspondingly deeper. Only confusion results when little children are told the meaning of words, outright, or are directed to their little dictionaries without further guidance. What does it mean to a little inner city child with an impoverished background to be told that a *wolf* is a wild animal, that a *churn* is a butter maker, that a *mountain* is an elevation of land?

For words to be used intelligently in communication, they must be learned on three sequential levels: by experiences; by verbalism; by conceptualization. First comes the real experience. When, for example, a child sees a wolf in a zoo, a churn in a museum, or a mountain in the country, he gets a real idea of these things. Since it's not always possible to make the acquaintance of real things, use plenty of pictures. Pictures reenforce these ideas. Then the words that go with these ideas, heard, repeated, read, and written, constitute the second level, that of verbalism. Lastly comes the conceptual level where, after many experiences, many pictures, and much practice in the use of the new word, the concept is formed. Then *wolf* has a real meaning, as does *churn* and *mountain.*

Help in sentence control will come easier than you think, if you appeal to the common sense of your children. Try them, for example, on cutting across the pedantic, stilted kind of sentences that appear frequently in the compositions of little children who are familiar only with the stilted sentences found in their readers.

Jennifer has a dog. The dog's name is Billy. Billy can bark. Billy can run. Billy can catch balls.

With the author's permission, write this piece on the board. Have it read aloud. Ask the children what they think.

Could anybody make it swing more? If nudges are necessary, call attention to the fact that there are five sentences in this composition. Can it be rewritten in four sentences? Try it! In three? Try again. And how grown up it sounds in two sentences:

> Jennifer has a dog named Billy. Billy can run and bark and catch balls.

Let them play with these two sentences. Perhaps they'd prefer to tell that story in one sentence? And yes, how very grown-up it sounds, to say:

> Jennifer's dog, Billy, can run and bark and catch balls.

How to Promote Functional Writing in the Upper Grades

With older children, you develop your writing program in the same way, but you work for more advanced writing techniques.

In *practical writing*, your children will have increasing opportunities for utilitarian experiences such as the production of committee reports, précis, blurbs and reviews. They will be writing articles for the class newspaper, abstracting material from their reference books, sending for information and developing charts for exhibition.

In *personal writing*, the same desire that motivated the younger children, the desire for personal involvement, continues to hold. Being older, they will be writing their autobiographies, reactions, diaries, accounts, tall stories, science fiction, joke books, plays and journals. And the closer they keep to writing what they know, what they feel and what they are, the better their writing will be, and the more convincing, no matter what their social and cultural level may be.

In a way, the promotion of personal and creative writing is the easiest subject in the curriculum. Here you do not have to pound away at facts, as in the social studies; you do not have to hammer for accuracy, as in number work; you do not have to drill for coordination, as in physical training. In the promotion of personal writing, you have only to draw on what's inside your children—their hopes and aspirations, their feelings, good humor and imagination.

It's not at all difficult to start your class on this kind of writing. A good topic, an enthusiastic teacher, and your children will be off and away! But unless you give them the wherewithal so *they can express themselves to their own satisfaction,* your writing program is doomed to failure, or at best, to a weekly theme that is dull and deadening and required. Avoid this demeaning state of affairs that takes no account of the built-in cache of drives and dreams that are there, within each of your children.

Give yourself and your children the happy reward of seeing progress, week by week, on paper after paper. And you can do it: (1) by equipping yourself with a long range plan for developing written expression, not just *having* written expression; (2) by equipping your children with the skills they need for evaluating their written results.

Five Steps and Three Writing Periods will provide your class with a good writing experience and some surprising improvement.

STEP 1: You motivate your class by way of an intriguing topic sparked by a quotation, a picture, a newspaper item, an exciting activity in another curriculum area. Motivation is any experience that starts your children thinking and talking. It is *not* an announcement by you that they are to write about an intriguing topic.

Suppose the time is September, and you are about to set your children to writing the first theme of the year. You are *not* going to ask them to write *How I Spent My Summer Vacation!* Instead, because you are going to involve them by engaging their emotions, you ask, "Was there anything you did this summer that you never thought you could learn to do in a hundred years?" And you let the children open the topic.

—One will have learned how to dive from a high board.
—One, how to be brave on a camping trip.
—One, how to catch a fish.
—One, how to hold her temper; how not to cry; how to set her hair.
—One, how to whistle through his fingers.

STEP 2: You ready your children for writing about the topic. If they are writing on *I Never Thought I Could Do It*, they need some help from you.

They need help with vocabulary so they can really tell it the way it happened. Draw these words from them, and you'll soon be listing words on the board that tell of wishful thinking, courage and cowardice, hesitation and persistence, disappointment, misery, embarrassment, more perseverance, and finally, glittering success.

They need help with sequence, and so you develop a number of guiding questions that you subsequently write on the board:

• Why did you think you never could do this thing?
• Why was it important to you?
• How did you feel when you tried and failed?
• How did success finally come to you?
• How did you feel at the moment of success?
• And then what happened?

They need help with ways of conveying the feeling-tone as well as the facts, which means help with vocabulary.

Throughout the discussion, keep a pad and pencil handy, and as the children talk about their determined endeavors, jot down some of their expressions so you can put them on the board later, when you want to point out that one way of conveying emotion is by variation in sentence length.

At the beginning of the discussion, when your children are talking about their frustrations, their sentences will be long and rambling:

John: Everybody in my family knew how to dive, but because I once had a cold and a few other things, they said I couldn't do it.

Mary: I always believed that crying was a good way to get what I wanted, but then I couldn't stop even when I tried.

Tom: I knew that Indian boys caught fish without expensive gear, so I was sure I could do it, too, but everybody laughed at me.

Toward the end of the discussion, when the children are recounting their victories, they will speak with verve and use short choppy sentences, shortened to five words, to three, and sometimes to one!

John: I did it! I stood on the diving board. I closed my eyes. I jumped! Splash!

Mary: I took a big breath. I batted my eyes. I did not cry! I smiled, instead.

Tom: The fish came closer. He rose to the bait. He swallowed the hook. I did it! Hurrah!

Before you leave Step 2, call attention to the exclamation points that denote excitement, and to the use of commas that make long sentences read sensibly. Then have your children write up rough drafts of their experiences, and your first period in personal writing will have started off in high gear.

STEP 3: The next day, after referring briefly to the vocabulary and the questions on the board, you stand by while the children write up the first good draft of their themes.

Standing by means that you are enthusiastically available all the time that the children are writing to help, advise and admire. Because of your peripatetic interest, your children will do their best. Errors will be fewer and papers neater.

It may take an extra day to correct all the papers, but don't call those red marks corrections because that could be shattering to some of your children. It's far better to emphasize the need for polishing, reminding them that the class needs polished themes for the next step.

STEP 4: You encourage and train your children in self-evaluation.

It is not enough to ask a child to tell what he thinks about his paper because this kind of question will bring only such vague answers as: I think it's pretty good . . . I guess I never was great in writing . . . It's too long—or too short —or too sloppy . . . It could be better.

And this is no kind of evaluation at all.

If you really want your children to view their work critically, develop a chart of specifics by which they can evaluate:

- Can they reorganize their material so that the incidents are noted in sequence, i.e., can they move a sentence from one place to another to make the meaning clearer?
- Can they find the best sentence in a piece of writing and defend it?
- Can they pinpoint the most interesting words in a paper?
- Can they judge whether the ending fits with the beginning?
- Can they proofread their papers and make the necessary corrections? And here, in the matter of proofreading, are a whole handful of minor but necessary specifics: the correct heading on the paper; the two skipped lines flanking the title; the two margins; the identation of the paragraph; the capitals at the beginning of each sentence; the omission of no words; the proper punctuation at the end of every sentence, meaning a period, a question mark, or an exclamation

point—and of course the correct spelling of every word.

A word about spelling, the red pencilling of which discourages so many children from writing. Most teachers encounter few problems when teaching spelling, and most children have even fewer problems in scoring high marks on their tests. But there are tests and tests. Tested in vertical columns on Friday, most words are correctly spelled, and most papers rate 100%. But tested horizontally, in sentences, many words are not correctly spelled and many papers do not rate anywhere near 100%. If you would give your children spelling power that stays with them, you will have to get them to learn at least five words and three shades of meaning for every word that you teach them.

Consider the word *move*—m-o-v-e—is that enough? No! if you teach *move*, your children can easily learn, then and there, to spell *moves, moved,* and *moving,* as well as *remove, removes, removed, removing* and *movable!* And, while they're doing that, get each one to reach back to his hidden cache of knowledge, add a word to the new spelling word, and you have an exercise in extended meaning with: *move* furniture, *move* troops, *move* mountains, and *move* the question!

Now, how many words and phrases can your children develop using the new word, *change?* (*Change* clothes, *change* minds, *change* trains and *change* money should intrigue them.) And what can they do with *square?* With *follow, swallow, arm* or *box?*

Check your manual, your spelling book and your dictionary for spelling rules. And then, when you present these rules to your children for the careful spelling of certain words, remember that your children will be making mistakes —never in the entire word, only in the hard part. So dramatize the hard parts and prevent the mistakes. Call attention to them by using colored chalk and bold printing on your chalkboard, in words:

- where there are silent letters as in *knit* and *knot*, *climb* and *thumb*.
- where there are double letters as in *swimming*, *whipping*, and *hitting*.
- where there are built-in mispronunciations or where the sounds are deceiving as in *"Br,* it's cold in the *library* in *February,"* and "Never *believe* a *lie."*

And then, you will, of course, reenforce the learning of spelling, routinely, by way of pertinent homework.

In class thereafter, particularly in the written composition periods, you will be seeing improvement in spelling. But don't ease off. Set up proofreading partners so that your children can proofread and edit each other's written work, and watch the facility in this area increase consciously and conspicuously.

And this brings you to the next step in your development of a good writing experience.

STEP 5: You lend importance to the written work by displaying it and thereby lend importance to the authors.

Post some of the papers on your hall bulletin board under the caption, MEET THE AUTHORS. Place some in the class book. File others away in folders for individual collections. And some, of course, may be read in the assembly, and so shared.

Throughout the year, as you promote written expression by way of your 5 Step Plan, keep powering your children with two-way techniques that will enable them better to express their ideas and feelings, more intelligently to evaluate themselves in the same ways that you will be evaluating them. And, since a writing activity promoted in this way takes at least three days, you would be wise to limit the writing to a page or a page and a half, at most.

And then the great day will come when your children will want to write long themes: stories, myths, mysteries. Good! Make a deal. Promise to show them how to plan a story, if they will promise to serialize it. And if they do that, you will be able to develop bite-sized story portions each week until the project is completed. And it's in these bite-sized portions that you will be furthering the development of tight writing techniques: the opening sentences that catapult the reader right into the action; the verbs that move the story; and the strong closing sentences that are virtual cliff hangers.

The ABCD Plan Will Ready Your Class for Story Writing and So You Start Them on the Writing of a Synopsis.

You give them an ABCD plan to hang their thinking on, with A for the Action that makes the story; B for the Background that the action takes place in; C for the Characters in it; and D for the Dialogue that delineates the characters.

Encourage discussion and lead it so that the class understands that this plan comes to life only in the presence of a strong conflict or an overpowering drive. Then help your children verbalize these conflicts and drives, take them through the five steps you've been using all along, and the resulting synopses will astound you.

Your children may then want to develop their synopses into three or four part stories, or they may choose to write altogether different synopses and develop them into lengthy stories, and if they do—more power to them!

In the meantime, and all the time, drive for brevity so that your children learn to use one sparkling word in place of many; a pithy phrase instead of a rambling sentence; a concise sentence instead of an interminable paragraph. And for this skill of brevity you need to develop lessons in cutting and pruning, and in using the most apt vocabulary.

Vocabulary Unlimited could serve as a slogan in your lively class! Sell your children on the importance of vocabulary because words are the foundation stones of your writing program. Only with rich and varied words will your children be able to express their thoughts and feelings with increasing precision.

So—learn to be a word opportunist in periods apart from your planned writing activities. And, as with younger children, develop vocabulary lists, in categories:

* Are your children studying about houses? Good! Post a picture on a chart, take your class for a walk, and see 10 or 15 different kinds of buildings in the neighborhood. Name these buildings on your chart. Also name the kinds of workers who built these houses and the tools they used. How many words might there be in such a category? 200 at the very least!
* Are your children reading about sailing ships in their basal readers? Splendid! Look at texts and encyclopedias and then appoint three committees to develop lists of words so that you can all talk and write intelligently about sailing ships!

Committee #1

Who works on a sailing ship?

What does he do?

Committee #2

Who helps build a sailing ship?

What materials would he have to get from the ship chandler?

Committee #3

How might the people on a sailing ship feel if they were:

In a fog? In a wild storm? Becalmed? Cast upon a strange island?

Use all kinds of occasions to develop all kinds of word lists.

It's Health Day in your school and you're checking eyes and ears? Great! Develop a detective's vocabulary for seeing and hearing! If it's a matter of seeing, how much more exciting it is to peer and peek, glance, discern and inspect, as well as to stare and squint and spy! As for listening— well, who wouldn't enjoy hearing about eavesdropping and harkening, heeding, apprehending and pricking up one's ears!

Such lists of words are fun and provide considerable enrichment, but for vocabulary power that really counts, your children need to understand how words are built. So use the functional approach, tie in with some other learning activity, and build vocabulary wherever you find a need and an opportunity; e.g., on any social studies level, there's always talk of commerce and trade, meaning talk about transportation. Stop right there and consider the root word, *port.* Coming from the Latin, *port* comes with two meanings: to carry, and a gate or an opening.

Can your children see how they might come up with a list of 50 words, using the root *port?* They'll start off with *portable* and *porter, export, deport, report, import.* They'll continue with *portal* and *portage* and *porthole*—and then you send them to the dictionaries for a real word hunt! Guided this way, your children will learn, remember and make good use of the building blocks that make up our language: the prefixes, the suffixes, and the roots.

But they have more—much more—to learn about vocabulary. New words are being coined every day because new things are invented every day, together with new machines and new occupations.

Fifty years ago, there was no such word as *zipper* and the richest millionaire couldn't have bought a zipper, no matter what. He couldn't have flown a *jet plane*, spoken to a *meter maid*, or hired a *television* repairman. These and hundreds more are all new words, as new as the the age we live in. And there are old words, too, bowing out of circulation, because the things these words stand for are bowing out of circulation. Today, you'd find it very hard to visit an *icehouse*, find a man wearing a *cravat*, ride in a *surrey*, buy a pair of *leggings*, or sleep in a *featherbed*.

Bring your children up to date in vocabulary! Set your girls to devising a *Handbook of the Newest Words from A to Z*, from *astronaut* to *zoom*, and set your boys to devising a *Handbook of Old Time Words*, also from A to Z, from *abacus* to *zeppelin*—two once proud words, now bowing out of our time!

It's true that the richest vocabulary and your most skillfully taught writing skills will not empower your children with creativity because creativity is not something that can be taught. But it's also true that a powerful vocabulary and vigorous writing techniques will release your children from the enervating custom of writing dull and deadly themes. So released, your children will more easily communicate their limitless ideas and personal feelings, simply, clearly and forcefully. And they will do so on a surprisingly high level.

5

Building an Exciting
Social Studies Program

Ask your class for a definition
of the social studies, and you may be surprised and morti-
fied. Some will have no idea at all. Some will guess that
social studies is: Pets, Clothing, Community Workers. Older
children, whose texts are clearly titled *Social Studies,* may
open to the Table of Contents and announce that social studies is the Age of Exploration!

And if this is what your children say, they haven't the
faintest notion what social studies is about.

In part, social studies is the study of people and places.
In greater depth, it is the study of the way people live and
have lived in given places; how they manage under geographical conditions of climate and terrain; how they change
their environment to suit themselves; how they utilize their
natural resources; how they fit into their biological biome;
and how they relate to each other economically and socially.
In reality, social studies is all this, PLUS. For your children,
this plus can contribute:

- added *meaning* to their required social studies;
- added incentive to *learning* the social studies *skills and practicing* them.

Four ways to add meaning to your social studies program

There are many ways to add meaning to your program. Here are four: relating the required study to your children's interests; practicing understanding; overcoming stereotypes; and reading historical fiction.

How to Relate the Required Study to Children's Interests

Any required topic can be tied to your children's interest in Today, and you can do this on any level, if you start with Today.

If the topic for your upper graders should be "Animals Around the World" with emphasis on their service to Man, you could begin in any number of ways:

- with the classification of animals from the one-celled protozoa that live in the sunlit seas, and together with the algae, provide the food base for marine life.
- with the domestication of the dog by Early Man.
- with an imaginary safari to the parklands of Africa.
- with newspaper accounts of a battle on the Senate floor concerning the current use of pesticides and their effect on animals.

Whether your children go on safari or investigate pesticides, they need a plan, and this plan may include the many kinds of animals, animals used for work, animals used for their products, ecological habitats necessary for the survival of animals, the food chain, and laws protecting animals. Your class will be surprised to learn that a farmer, dusting his apple orchard with a guaranteed pesticide, may be responsible for the death of hundreds of birds in his county because birds eat insects that eat pesticide. And your children will be shocked to learn that this same dusting operation could cause the death of fish in a lake 100 miles downstream. So started, you will have little difficulty in guiding your children's interest.

With younger children, you can begin the same study of animals around the world and their service to Man, on a closer-to-home scale. Again, with emphasis on Today, you start with pets, and you plan two good motivating questions such as:

Who is the most important animal in your life?

What good are animals?

The idea that they themselves are animals and therefore most important of all, will be an intriguing thought. Now open the topic to include other animals.

YOU are two-legged animals. Right? Right!

Can you think of any other two-legged animals? (and you list the children's answers on the board.)

Are there any other kinds? Four-legged? Six-legged? Eight-legged? No-legged? And how about centipedes and millepedes? (And the list on the board grows longer!)

It grows longer *and* longer because there are so many different kinds of animals. And almost every kind that is not ferocious is likely to be a pet to some child, some place in the world.

Indeed, there is so much to learn about such intriguing pets that your children are sitting on the edges of their chairs, aglow with anticipation, eager to learn, waiting for teacher to teach them.

Warning! Don't disappoint your children. You cannot teach what you do not know. You must know a lot to be able to teach them a lot. And since none of us is expert in every area of the curriculum, check your knowledge of this topic right away. Go through the course of study, the textbooks, the supplementary books, the reference books and filmstrips that are available to your grade in your school. Then familiarize yourself with the picture files, recordings and trade books in the public library. Don't be surprised if you find as many as 20 or 30 such trade books on your topic, because today's libraries are remarkably well stocked.

Don't listen to colleagues, no matter how well meaning they may be, who advise you to draw up a ditto sheet of animals, tell your children about them, and move to the next topic. *Telling isn't teaching!* Teaching is firing children to learn, and guiding them in their learning which is a very personal finding-out process. And no one ever put this better than Lincoln Steffens, when he said, "I teach my children and tell all others."

End of sermon—And now, back to the unit on animals.

If you follow this approach, your next step with your class is a trip to the zoo. Then a trip to a farm, and then you are ready to ask your second question, "What good are animals?" And for this question, your children need information. So you take them to the library, having first alerted the librarian so that she is prepared with a supply of assorted, easy-reading animal books. And immediately, your motivated children will want to adopt an animal apiece, to learn about! This might be a pet of their own, or an animal they admired in the zoo or at the farm. Think, then, of the exciting reading ahead of them, as they check out the habits and characteristics of these animals in their library books and Junior Reference materials.

Consider, for example, the characteristic of locomotion, and you have the idea for a smashing bulletin board. Title? HOW DO ANIMALS GET FROM PLACE TO PLACE? Well, how do they? Cows lumber. Ducks waddle. Ponies trot. Horses gallop. (So horses are good for racing!) And pigeons fly. (So some, the homing kind, are good as messengers!)

Treat the matter of vocal communication in the same manner. Dogs bark, so they are good for guarding property and alerting owners. Canaries sing, so they are good for entertaining homebound invalids. Other animals possess other attributes, so help your children explore the attributes of their chosen animals. Findings? Some animals are good for eating, some for working, some for entertaining, some for loving, and all for their part in natures scheme of things.

When each child's research is done, and the individual "My Animal Booklet" completed, what a treat in store for your class as all the booklets are read and reread. And this will be a never-to-be-forgotten treat because the work that went into these booklets was meaningful in a hardworking, personal way, and the knowledge acquired, then selected and adapted for inclusion in the booklets, was amazing in scope and depth.

But actually, this sort of heartwarming achievement is not amazing at all—not when a teacher prepares herself as you prepared yourself *before* you began to develop this unit with your children.

How to Practice Understanding

In social studies, understanding pivots on the children's learning how, and in what manner they relate to other people and to the world around them. When they are very young, their world is the immediate family. Later, relatives and friends are included. Still later, all children, in varying degrees, become aware of other people in the neighborhood and the school. When they are considerably older, their relationship with other people in other places and other times, comes into focus by direct involvement or by vicarious experience through the media.

The relationship of a child to the world about him cannot be brushed aside. At every step of the way, somebody beyond his immediate family makes it possible for him to be clothed and fed and cared for. He wears a woolen suit? Somebody far away had to raise the sheep and shear them. Somebody had to card the wool and spin it into cloth. Somebody had to tailor the cloth and fashion it into a suit. Somebody had to make the thread, the buttons, the lining, the zipper and the sewing machine. Somebody had to transport these things by train and truck. Somebody had to provide the store and stand by to sell. Somebody had to provide the money to buy that suit. And somebody even had to manufacture the money!

And so you build awareness and understanding of the fact that every child is served by many people. You use books and pictures and trips and walks as you build this understanding into and of the things all around: the milk your children drink during recess; the window pane they look through; the grassy field they romp in; the paved street they skate on; and the skates, of course!

This kind of awareness, however, is one-sided, whereas life is not. If people serve your children, your children have an obligation to return something. This is the message of your social studies, as you build civic understanding, and here's how you can do this in your consideration of one topic after another:

Take the Topic of Community Workers

You plan carefully to make sure your children know and appreciate the obvious community workers: the policeman, fireman, milkman, and sanitation man, as well as the welfare lady, the minister and the teacher. With equal care, you develop understanding concerning the services of these workers to the community. Splendid! Now, help your children practice that understanding by practicing appreciation!

You can do this by developing two kinds of Experience Charts: one about the services these workers perform; the other, about their living patterns. The living pattern of the fireman, for example, includes periodic stints of night duty. Well, then, Mr. Fireman must, periodically, sleep during the day. And Mrs. Fireman gets very cross if children play noisy games in her street when her husband is sleeping. When your children understand the situation and can refrain from their noisy games, they are practicing not only understanding but appreciation of the fireman.

Take the Topic of Families

In the same way, when studying *families*, young children can learn that all the families in your class have children, but that not all the children have a full complement of adults living in the same house. Some may have fewer. Some may have a couple of extras in the form of grandparents, aunts, uncles, or long-time house guests. Again, you will want to develop two kinds of Experience Charts: one in terms of "Who lives in my house"; the other, in terms of "Everybody in my house has a job." It would also be a good idea to help the children devise their own experience charts, because each child's family is different in size and color, income, background, interests and the like. (See Chapter 1, p. 27 for ways of decorating charts with family cutouts.)

Now, what understandings do these individual Experience Charts and individual family cutouts lead to? That all families started with two parents? That is correct. That some families continue to have two parents and that other families, for a number of reasons, change? That is also correct!

You can add still more meaning to the composition of each family by focusing on the age of the children in each of the family units. This you can do by way of individual bar graphs.

Even for primary graders, nothing could be easier than making and interpreting bar graphs, because they are already familiar with picture graphs, and if they aren't, display and discuss a few with your class. And, they already know the number line, which is one of the first things they learn in math. So draw a large scale number line on your board that looks like this:

0-1-2-3-4-5-6-7-8-9-10

Then upend another number line on the left, so that together, the two number lines look like this:

```
10
 9
 8
 7
 6
 5
 4
 3
 2
 1
 0  1  2  3  4  5  6  7  8  9  10
```

The idea of a graph will almost automatically fall into place if you transfer these two number lines to a 3′ by 4′ sheet of graph paper. Now show the children how to plot simple information in the form of a bar graph, on this large sheet of graph paper. Show them how to make up a bar graph for a family that has three children. And so you start with Janie, age nine, whose brother Tommy is seven, and whose sister, Maria, is four. Since Janie is the oldest, she's #1 on the graph. Tommy is #2, and Maria is #3. You explain that the numbers on the vertical line represent years, and you explain the numbers on the horizontal line represent children, and so Janie's graph will look like the one depicted in Figure 6.

Can the class plot Cathy's graph? There are only two children in this family: Cathy, eight, and Freddie, three.

There are six children in Gordon's family, and starting with the oldest, they are: Jerry, ten; Frank, nine; Gordon, eight; Terry, six; Melvin, four; and Nora, one. And of course, the class can do it!

Now look around for a family whose oldest child is above ten, so you can explain that the vertical line as well as the horizontal line need not indicate a progression of one

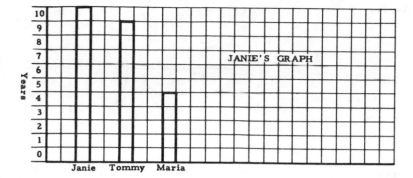

Figure 6

every time, but may be set up to represent units of two or five or ten, or more than ten, as the case may be. When the children grasp that, they will be able to plot all kinds of information for the class: daily class attendance, milk consumption, indoor and outdoor temperature and personal scores in games!

Take the Topic of Money

Added meaning and understanding need not be restricted to the social studies units. Put meaning into money the next time you plan a class trip! If, for example, the children have been saving a dollar for an all-day excursion, how shall this money best be spent?

Three or four circle graphs will provide more immediate understanding than days of discussion. So which plan (*Figure 7*) is your class likely to accept?

Apply the skill of graph making to your children's personal problems. If some seem to be short on homework time, help them organize the 24 hours on a pictorial circle graph. If others run out of spending money in no time flat, a circle graph will clarify the kinks in the budget!

When children learn to make graphs, they also learn to read graphs, and this kind of reading is a most important

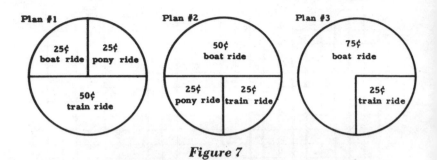

Figure 7

social studies asset in the upper grades. Then information that would require hours of digging is grasped at a glance. A bar graph conveys instant information concerning the size of cities, business indices, political trends and unemployment factors. A circle graph pictures the allocation of the tax dollar, the deployment of servicemen, the racial balance in the country. If they look at a graph with understanding, the message comes through and the meaning is clear.

But suppose they look at people? What's the message that comes through if these people are black or brown, red, yellow, or white? What's the message if they wear Oriental garb, or African or Indian?

Too often, the message is a great big stereotype!

How to Overcome Stereotypes

"A stereotype," according to the Random House Dictionary, "is a simplified and standardized conception or image invested with special meaning, and held in common, by members of a group. The cowboy and the Indian are American stereotypes."

Consider the stereotype of the American Indian. The occasion? The final wrap-up of your Indian Unit, and your committees are ready.

* My report is about Indian squaws and braves and maidens.

- Ours is about Indian war dances.
- Tom and I will tell about the peace pipe ceremonies and we have pictures to show.
- I will explain the Rain Dance and I have a record to play.
- And we will demonstrate, "What's Cooking in that Indian Kettle."
- And I'm going to read part of a very famous poem about Indians, by Longfellow.

"But first," your nine-year-old chairman announces, "a message from our sponsor, the Museum! For nothing at all, you may come and see lifelike and lifesize exhibits of Indians!

"For a few pennies, you may buy picture postcards showing authentic Indian scenes. If you have more money, you can buy paperback books about Indian Lore and Legend. And if you have about a dollar, you can order souvenir tomahawks or necklaces or moccasins—genuine souvenirs, straight from a genuine Indian Reservation!

"Don't wait! Order today and become an expert tomorrow! And to help you, here is your free Indian Brochure, with the compliments of this committee."

And it's a splendid brochure. You can only imagine the many hours that went into its making: visiting the museum, collecting leaflets and reading library books, to say nothing of the secret help given by trusted mothers who ran the ditto machine.

Carried away by the excellence of the committee reports, and by your pedagogical enthusiasm, you determine, privately, to visit an Indian Reservation on your next summer holiday.

Don't go if you want to avoid disappointment. The reports you have just heard belong to long ago. The "now" of Indian life is vastly different. And the "now" definitely belongs in your Indian Unit, or else you are perpetuating a mythical picture, a romanticized stereotype of Indian life, and picturing Indians as simple children of nature.

Needed in your class is a committee charged to explore Indian life, today. And this involves more trips to the museum and library, more digging for filmstrips and slides, pictures and books, newspaper and magazine articles, showing: Indian Life as it is lived on the reservations, today; schools and social activities of today; work opportunities and houses, today; and the financial and social problems of the Indians, today! .

Needed, too, is a committee to look into Pen Pal opportunities for exchanging letters with Indian children, and another committee to try to locate a real live Indian, who, for a very small fee, might visit the class and tell about Indian life, today!

Background, legend and lore are the ingredients of history, but don't stop with history. Make history live by cutting away the stereotypes. And you can do this by helping your children relate their history to the living excitement that surrounds them today; and by encouraging them to read widely, so that they neither develop stereotypes, nor perpetuate them.

Wide reading will provide your children with a storehouse of exciting facts. So look around your classroom and check out your book inventory.

* Have you the newest, most recently written social studies texts?
* Have you multi-level texts that are based on multi-level vocabularies for easy reading by your slower children, and for more advanced reading by your more advanced children?
* Have you multi-ethnic texts dealing with the histories, problems and contributions of multi-ethnic groups?

If you have these texts, that's good but not great. If you don't have them, that's no great tragedy, either. Texts, even five or six different kinds (and whose classroom could store that many sets of books?) provide only five or six different titles. And, if you limit your teaching to five or six titles, you'll be limiting your children's learning!

If it's stereotypes you want to break, then your children need unlimited reading and learning from an unlimited number of books in order to get background material, with period atmosphere, and with admirable characters to emulate. In this way, they will be able to get a more realistic understanding of the social studies. And nothing will further this understanding more powerfully, than the reading of historical fiction, a most enjoyable activity and a happy possibility, since you live within hailing distance of a public library system.

How to Profit from the Reading of Historical Fiction

Unlike the reading of the social studies texts, the reading of historical fiction is an experience in pure pleasure and pays off with three unexpected dividends:

(1) It makes the period being considered come to life so that the reader knows what kind of home the hero had; what his family was like; how they spent the 24 hours of the day; what problems—personal, environmental, social and racial—they had to overcome; what qualities of character were necessary for survival; and how the hero embodied these qualities.

(2) It underscores the universality of the problems of man as he strives with his environment and his fellowmen. Whether the time is 1500 or 1900 or today, man tries to support his family and fights to protect what is his, or what he believes should be his.

(3) It enables the reader to identify himself with the emotional experiences of the people he's reading about, and he will remember these emotions long after he's forgotten the title of the book.

Your children may be reluctant readers, content with picture books, comic books, or no books at all. Your job is to sell them on historical fiction and to catapult them into other times and other places, and to immerse them in powerful vicarious experiences.

One Way to Sell Interest in a Single Book of Historical Fiction

You sell interest by being a good saleswoman, meaning that you select a gripping story and read just enough of it to your children so they want more—then lend the book to one, and place the names of the other eager children on a waiting list. You follow the same procedure for the next four or five days, each day "selling" another book of historical fiction that you've especially selected for high interest-low reading level.

Concurrently, you plan for wider selling and wider reading:

You arrange to borrow 40 or 50 books of historical and period fiction from the school and public library, being as careful as you can be to make sure that there's something suitable for each of your children: advanced books, easy books, picture books, and books that tell how the children of long ago solved personal problems.

You surprise your children by placing two of these books on each desk, before they come into the room at one o'clock.

You suggest they get acquainted with these books, and then read the one they like.

Your reluctant readers, inexperienced in the judging of new books will ask—How can anyone tell if he's going to like a book before he reads it? So you show them!

How to Preview a Book

In one exciting period, you can equip your class with a lifelong skill as you show each child how to:

Look first at the title of the book for clues about the content.

Look at the author's name. Children develop passionate attachments to favorite authors and will read anything he's written. So call attention to the authors you've read from the previous week, and some children will immediately feel special because they're holding a book by a now familiar name.

Read the blurb on the front flap of the bookjacket to see if the story appeals.

Read the criticism on the back of the bookjacket, to see what other people say about this book.

Read the first page or two of the book to see if it's interesting, understandable, easy to get into, and makes you want to read more.

And that's it! That's the way, you tell your children, to find out if they are going to like a book before they read it!

Steep your children in the reading of historical fiction, and when it takes, you would do well to reduce other homework assignments in favor of heavy reading in this area. It isn't necessary, you know, to make all the activities in the school day, concurrently, high-powered frontal attacks, participatory group experiences, or challenging assignments.

From the reading of historical fiction, your children will gain many concepts that cannot be taught, but can only be developed by the children on their own. Take for example, the concept that there is not one, but many histories of any given time and place:

To Mary, it may be the history of explorers and map makers; to John, it may be the military strategy of that very same era; to Dick, it may be the history of the frontier people as the frontier continued to move westward and left them behind; to Erik, the wild creatures of the surrounding forest are important; Janet sees history in the fashions, hair styles and quilting parties of the times; Jeremiah is entranced by the words and speech patterns of the locality; and Velda sees history in terms of her own race.

Only wide reading in historical fiction will people other times and other places for your children with authentic background material. It will also catch them up in a kaleidoscope of universal feelings experienced by the pioneers in their drive to get ahead.

And you don't reduce the pressure in this area. You keep praising and guiding and encouraging your children to make full use of the library, till they are "hooked" for life on the reading of historical fiction.

Soon, soon, your children will be able to move into the area of independent reading and independent work. And this will have happened because you moved the center of incentive for learning from the teacher to the students—from teachermade assignments to student involvement.

But this bubbling incentive for learning in your class will continue to bubble only as long as your children continue to succeed on their own in independent work, so don't allow their exciting plans to fall flat. Counter such a dim possibility by empowering them with three study skills!

**Three study skills to reenforce incentive
for independent learning**

Help your children acquire these overlapping study skills so that they know where to locate sources for information, how to run-down specific information in these sources, and how to extract this information from the print.

WHERE TO LOCATE SOURCES FOR INFORMATION

Children often believe that the most important thing about school is the remembering of facts. Of course facts are important, because with facts they have something to think with, in order to analyse and compare. But an educated person knows more than facts. He knows *where* to find the facts he needs!

For children on any level, the basic academic sources for facts are printed reference materials and the graphic materials found in newspapers, magazines, and authoritative tradebooks.

So consider the kind of information that's wanted. Then consider the source where your children are most likely to find the information they want. And you start with the many reference materials in your room: the dictionary, atlas, maps and globes, almanacs, encyclopedias, and telephone books.

The first thing to learn, because children do not automatically know this, is the fact that specific information is to be found in specific reference materials. This means that your children need help in learning how to find their way among these many references, and so you might:

(1) Appoint committees of three or four; give each committee one of the references and 15 minutes, to find out what amazing questions they could answer with the aid of this particular reference.

(2) Call on the committees at the end of the allotted time, to report on their findings. Being temporary experts now, they will soon make it clear that each reference does indeed serve a particular purpose, and that, accordingly words are defined in the dictionary; places are located in the atlas; comparative geographical facts are indicated on maps and globes; current facts and statistics are compiled in the almanac; personal, business and postal data is noted in the telephone book; and a run-down of almost any topic may be found in the encyclopedia.

(3) Permit brief browsing so as to introduce the look and feel and purpose of each of these references to your children.

(4) Assign homework, asking the children to make up six very hard questions, indicating the kind of reference that would be most likely to contain the answer.

This kind of procedure, backed with plenty of practice, is excellent training for locating information, but don't limit your children's learning to the instructional materials in your room. There are quicker and surer ways of locating information that is up to the minute! For instant information about *now*, introduce your children to the commonplace graphics that busy people use: road maps and weather maps, charts, tables and graphs. Your busy children can obtain this same material from newspapers and magazines, business releases and government publications.

Knowing *where* to locate information is certainly an important skill. It's equally important to know *how* to run down a specific bit of information, down to the exact page and paragraph, and then to know how to interpret it.

HOW TO RUN DOWN INFORMATION IN PRINTED REFERENCES AND GRAPHICS

Now that your children know the specific purpose of each of your seven references, show them how to *pinpoint information:*

Check out with them the seven points involved in the organization of most study books. If your class is shaky, provide practice in the readers, the math, social studies and science texts. In each instance, the seven points refer to the title page, the table of contents, the chapter headings and sub-headings, the maps, charts, graphs and index.

When your children are thoroughly familiar with this seven-way make-up of most of their texts, help them discover the fact that the large, important looking reference books are organized in the same manner. This will be a satisfying bit of knowledge, but it will not of itself enable them to find the information they want efficiently and with dispatch. So—

Ground your children in functional fact-finding skills. Start them off to certain success in the use of the table of contents and the index.

Here are three pointers that are too often taken for

granted, but which your children need to know about the table of contents:

(1) Its location. It's always in front of the book.

(2) Its arrangement. It shows the organization of the subject matter: according to topics in the English texts; according to chronology in the social studies books; according to location and topography in the geography books; and according to units in the science books.

(3) Its use. The table of contents shows the page location of the general topics, and indicates the scope of the book.

Whereas the table of contents lists general topics, the index indicates the exact location of specific items. So here are six checks for gauging competence in the use of the index:

(1) Do your children know where to find the index? It is usually at the back of the book, although it may appear on colored pages elsewhere, and in encyclopedias the index for the entire set is often found either in the first or the last volume.

(2) Do they know how to alphabetize to the third and fourth letter, and how to apply this knowledge to finding facts in the index?

(3) Do they know how to recognize the different kinds of indexes—the straight away alphabetical listing of facts, and the alphabetical listing of facts under alphabetically listed major topics?

(4) Do they know how to pick out the key word in an assignment in order to locate it in the index?

(5) Do they know how to read the index in terms of mechanics—dark print, punctuation marks, transposed word order?

(6) Do they know how to read the index for cross references? And if they don't know, there's only one thing to do. Teach them!

In addition to checking out the printed references, teach your children how to check out the graphic materials. Graphics, in the form of charts and tables, maps and graphs, are actually abstractions that contain concentrated information. To interpret graphics, your children need to learn the meaning of the pertinent symbols, the colors and shapes, the progression of figures, and the specialized terminology.

Then, guide them in the making of their own graphics! Such practice will enable them to interpret the printed graphics with greater competency. And soon your current events periods will sparkle with information that was almost effortlessly and automatically lifted from the newspaper graphics!

Little by little, step by step, you'll find your children growing in power. In addition, they'll be able to locate the source of almost any challenging topic in one of their printed references. They'll be able to run down even obscure facts in the index, and turn to the exact page. Then what?

What will they be able to do with this newly found information, so excitingly presented on the pages? They could read it, of course, but then they'd forget most of it. They could copy it, but that would take forever, and then they'd only have to read it again in order to refresh their memories. And, if they are using several references, the study problem is altogether compounded.

How to Extract Information from the References

The thing to do, when information has been properly located, is to get it out of the books and into the heads. And your children can do this by outlining what they read, in an organized and orderly manner. (See Chapter 3 for ways of developing competence in outlining.)

With a clear outline, your children can see at a glance what the selection is about. And a clear outline will enable them to test themselves minutely. All they have to do is turn every heading and subheading of the outline into a question, and see if they can back up their answers with supporting facts!

This, then, is one way to organize a social studies program:

to provide *added meaning* and *practice in understanding* as in the study of community workers, families, and money;

to *overcome stereotypes*, as in the unit on Indians; and to further the *reading of historical fiction.*

And, since such a program entices children into independent work, it calls for efficient study habits, for learning how to *locate sources* of information; learning how to *run down the specifics* of information; and learning how to *extract the information* from the printed pages of texts, references and newspapers.

Involved in such an exciting program, your children, at the end of the year, will not hesitate when you ask them for a definition of social studies!

6

Establishing Unique Ways to Study
Science—Through Observation
and Experimentation

There's a natural tendency for teachers to rely heavily on textbooks, and many of today's texts are indeed exciting. They are often well organized, attractively illustrated, and accompanied by excellent Teacher's Guides. If new books are available, alert teachers want them. If the going gets tough, they don't hesitate to request them. And then notes like the following begin to appear on the principal's desk.

> TO . . . . . . The Principal
> FROM . . . Miss A, Classroom Teacher
>
> You asked for a strong science program, but my children are completely disinterested and will not learn! Please let me have 30 new textbooks and 30 new workbooks, and I will do my best to cover the topics.

While it is true that children who are not interested will not learn, it is also true that textbooks and workbooks are not primary factors in getting children interested. This observation applies particularly to the study of science, because science starts with "why," and so do children. A hundred times a day, children wil ask "Why?" "How?" "What happens when . . . ?"

Children ask questions because they are curious about their environment. But they don't want to *hear* the answers. Tell them, and they don't listen. Tell them again, and they become bored. They want to get into the act and find out for themselves.

And you can help them do just that. When you plan your mandated course of study, make sure you involve your children in finding-out experiences.

Experience is the best teacher

But finding out is a great skill, with rules and procedures of its own. It's a skill that's based on physical as well as mental experiences.

As a teacher, you may find it difficult to develop such experiences, but your children won't. They practice the skill of finding out almost every time they play.

Watch Carol playing Doctor in the Doll Corner: She wants to find out what's wrong. She examines her doll. She observes the symptoms: stiff arm, warm forehead, no pulse. She comes to a conclusion about the illness. She uses appropriate materials (real or imaginary).

Later, when the doctor examines a crying Carol, he says, "Let's find out what's the matter." He examines Carol. He observes the swollen hand, the reddened skin, the small scratch. He compares the swollen hand with the good hand. He concludes the situation is not serious, but requires aid. He uses the necessary materials: alcohol, a cotton swab, a hypodermic needle, an antibiotic.

Six rules for finding out

Carol at play, and the doctor in his examination, each followed the six basic rules of investigation:

- They tried to find out something.
- They examined the patients.
- They observed the situation, looking for facts.
- They compared the facts.
- They came to a conclusion.
- They used appropriate materials.

These six rules work in any kind of investigation. They work for the FBI. They work for detectives. They work for scientists in their laboratories. And they will work for you.

A way to capitalize on curiosity

Start the term by collecting the questions that children raise, and if they don't, encourage them to do so. Discuss these questions briefly with your class, then select one for immediate investigation. Put the other questions into a question box or transfer them onto a "We Want to Know" chart. Something like the following:

We want to know

Why do we draw the shades in this room every morning?

How can you tell what's in a bag without looking?

What would happen if you put a plant in a closet for a week?

Why does a balloon get smaller in a refrigerator?

Make certain that the question you select for this first finding-out activity: is provocatively interesting to the children; lends itself to experiential development; requires only simple materials; can be concluded in a few days.

Suppose you and the class want to find out "Why we have to put more water into the fish tank every Friday."

Make curiosity work for you

Now you need a plan for finding out. Here is a plan that starts with three questions you write on the chalkboard, and ends with a written experience chart made up of the six basic rules for finding out.

Your questions are:

1. What do we want to find out?
2. How can we do it?
3. What materials will we need for this investigation?

Let the children verbalize the many facets of the original problem. If we have to put more water in the tank every Friday, what happened to the water that was there last Friday? How could water disappear? If a committee watched day and night, would they be able to see the water disappearing? Would water disappear from every fish tank? Would it make a difference if one tank was covered, and one tank was *not* covered? *Let's find out!*

You will need two medium sized tanks, and you will need to fill them ¾ full.

Cover one tank with a pane of glass. Leave the other tank uncovered.

Do this on a Friday afternoon, and mark the water level on the side of each tank with a grease pencil.

Have the children observe the water level and mark it on the side of each tank every afternoon for a week.

Compare the markings on the sides of the tank the next Friday afternoon. The level in the covered tank will be the same as it was at the beginning of the week. The level of water in the uncovered tank will be lower!

Conclusion? Water disappears from an uncovered tank. That's why we have to add water every Friday afternoon. *We found out!*

Ways of extending learning

Where did the water go?

If your children are little, you simply tell them that the water disappeared into the air.

If your children are older, you pursue the *how* of this disappearance. Then you find yourself launched on the topics of water and water vapor and the water cycle—all prescribed topics in your course of study.

Young or old, all children learning science need to learn the vocabulary of science. In this instance, make certain that they learn the meaning of: *Evaporation,* liquid water changing to water vapor; *control,* which is a check on the experiment. In this experiment, the covered tank served as a check, for purposes of comparison.

Now your plan calls for an experience chart, so you and the children may summarize the entire finding-out activity by way of six basic steps, and it looks like this:

1. What we wanted to find out
2. What we did
3. What we observed
4. What materials we used
5. What we compared
6. What we found out

* What new words we learned in science

This chart, properly filled out with the aid of the children, serves as a review for the class, and as a record of an experiential activity.

In the primary grades, you and your children may develop so many experience charts in the course of the year that you will be able to fasten them together into a large, "We found out" chart book. Then the children may want to donate this book to the school library.

Older children, beyond the experience chart stage, will need to be instructed in the keeping of personal notebooks in science. In these notebooks, they will record their finding-out activities, more formally and in greater detail, but still in terms of the six basic steps:

1. Aim (What we want to find out)
2. Method (What we do)
3. Materials (What things we use)
4. Observation (What we learn by way of the five senses. What happens. How we keep records)
5. Comparison (With the control)
6. Conclusion (What we found out)

   * New Vocabulary

You look ahead

Not only is it important to capitalize on children's curiosity and to start with finding-out questions, it's also important to know where you are going in science. If you know where you're going, you can cue these bubbling questions into your overall plan for the year.

So—examine your course of study.

There are just so many mandated topics and just so many months in the average school year. Chart a one page time-table for yourself. Make it clear. Make it concise. Make it look like this:

Month	Topic	Topic	Topic	Topic
September				
October				
November				
December				
January				
February				
March				
April				
May				
June				

Later, as you approach each topic, you will plan in greater detail. In the meantime, your one page overview will show you that on any grade level, your science program, varying only in degree of emphasis, is indeed a study of the (natural) environment.

And you look around

There are many ways to study the environment. Experience may be the best teacher, but you, as a classroom teacher, will find it profitable to use other methods at times. Your approach will depend on your purpose.

You may plan science demonstrations or directed class experimentation. You may plan lessons in the use of textbooks and other reference materials. You may plan wide and varied use of the multi-media.

A good way to get a running start into the study of the environment is by way of neighborhood trips.

How to launch the study of the natural environment

Two or three neighborhood trips, the first month of the term, will launch you and your children on the study of the natural environment, and here's how to do it:

Develop the concept with your children that all things in nature are either living or non-living. Plants and animals (including people) are living things. Rocks, water, air and soil are non-living.

Elicit the fact that countless living and non-living things are to be found in the neighborhood. Ask how many of these natural things the children think they could find.

A camera trip nets pictures!

Plan a couple of photographic trips. Encourage the widespread use of cameras, and let the parents come along and help. You are going to take pictures of living things and of non-living things in your neighborhood!

Go to the school yard. Look at the cement. Any cracks in the cement? Look near the stone walls. Anything growing? Weeds? Grass? Wild flowers? Any moss? Any mold? Any little piles of leaves and sand? Any worms in the piles? Any trees? Cocoons in the trees?

Take all kinds of pictures!

Go on a trip along the nearby streets. Any rain gutters with plants growing in them? Any sidewalk cracks? How many plants and animals live there? Any trees? Take pictures of five different kinds of trees. Be sure to get the shape of the tree, the kind of bark and leaves, the leaf patterns. Any signs of animals living in these trees? Birds? Insects? Squirrels? Spiders?

Take pictures!

Adopt a tree and plan to take pictures of it in September, December, April and June.

Are there any hedges? Any seeds blown into the hedges? Any grass, weeds, bushes? How many different kinds of grass leaves can you find growing in one grassy spot?

Are there any parks nearby, or empty fields? Any swamps or little ponds you can see? What plants and animals live in the water? Algae? Water lilies? Fish? What plants and animals can you find alongside the edges of the swamp or pond? Ferns? Frogs? Snails?

Take pictures!

The pictures can all be classified!

This photographic round of neighborhood trips will result in a hundred pictures. Post them all, indiscriminately. Now, help your children learn the skill of classification, and if you have older children, you can develop this skill in considerable depth.

Ask which pictures seem to go together.

The children will suggest:

LIVING THINGS	NON-LIVING THINGS

After the children have divided all the pictures into these two categories, ask them to look at the pictures again, with a more critical eye. Ask whether they could classify them further. They will, and your chalkboard will begin to look like this:

LIVING THINGS	NON-LIVING THINGS
Plants	Rocks
Animals	Water
	Air
	Soil

If your children are upper graders, you can develop the skill of classification in considerable depth.

Animals may be classified as:

Vertebrates—mammals
             birds
             reptiles
             amphibians
             fish

Invertebrates—insects
           spiders
           crustaceans

Plants may be classified as:

Algae
Fungi
Mosses
Ferns
Evergreens
Flowering plants

What a beautiful and scientifically classified picture display you will have on your bulletin board! And these will be pictures that the children and their parents had taken on neighborhood walks—with their own cameras!

It's time to turn to the books

By this time, your children will experience a definite need for the textbook. So many questions need to be answered in detail. So many pictures need to be identified further.

So consider the textbook with your class. Be sure to study the Teacher's Guide, then study the Table of Contents. It will reveal chapters on plants and animals, rocks and water, soil and air. It will reveal chapters on the forces that affect living things: the forces of weather and gravity, of magnetism and light and sound. Correlate these chapters with the one-page-overview that you made of your science course of study.

Do you now settle down with your children and "dig" the textbook? No. You go on another trip and dig the roadsides and empty lots, a green field or a marshy area. This time you go on a collecting trip. This time, the children see and touch and handle the living and non-living things they will be reading about in their chapter or chapters for the week.

No cameras on a collecting trip! Instead, each child will need to bring along:

a plastic bag	a tape measure or ruler
rubber bands	a net
a plastic jar with	a notepad and pencil
a cover	a hand lens

And the teacher will need to bring along:

a couple of buckets	field guide of local plants
a compass	field guide of local animals
two or three spades	paper towels
grease pencils	wet paper towels in a plastic
adhesive tape	bag

Caution!

You don't blithely say, "This is a collecting trip," and go. That way lies grief and poison ivy, skinned knees and trouble with the neighbors.

You draw up a code of behavior with the children. You assign buddies, so no one gets lost. You devise a teacher-made rexographed map, that's pretty realistic because you've already scouted the area and you indicate directions, suggestions, and cautions by way of a legend (*Figure 8*). And you *make certain that the children can read the map!*

Later, back in the classrom, it will be necessary to organize the collection and complete the labeling.

Rocks may be labeled with inked adhesive tape, and jars may be labeled with grease pencils. Identification of plants and animals may be checked in the textbooks and field guides.

A laboratory in every classroom

If you haven't already done so, this is the time to turn a portion of your room into a laboratory. And this is the time to put to the test the two key words which characterize

Figure 8

1 *Dig here and collect specimens*
2 *Look under rocks and collect more specimens*
3 *Go no farther than this point*
4 *Rare plants here. Do NOT pick*
5 *Watch out for poison ivy*
6 *Step no farther along this edge*
7 *Stay this side of the stone fence*

all scientific activity. The two key words are *order* and *organization*, so:

PROVIDE A SCIENCE CORNER WITH:

- A shelf for science books, texts and references and nature study materials, how-to books, science biographies and a science dictionary.
- A science table, with a challenge-for-the-week on it.

If the class had been studying the interdependence of living things, you may want to exhibit a stuffed owl, borrowed from the local Museum of Natural History, or a good, clear picture of an owl, under the caption, WOULD YOU OR WOULD YOU NOT, LIKE TO HAVE AN OWL FOR A PET? WHY?

* A science table for children's exhibits, with a posted "We Take Turns Exhibiting Every Week" chart. An individual or group exhibit in the fall might contain a collection of assorted birds' nests, each labeled, and with the weight noted. Each weight might be accompanied by a picture of the bird that made it, and a notation of the bird's weight, which might be checked in a science encyclopedia. An individual or group exhibit might contain a collection of science toys with reports (posted on the wall behind), titled, "What Makes this Toy Work."

PROVIDE A BULLETIN BOARD FOR STIMULATING INTEREST

You might hang three differently shaped magnets on the bulletin board under the question, WHAT CAN THESE MAGNETS DO? And provide (posted on the bulletin board) an envelope with slips of paper for the answers.

PROVIDE A BULLETIN BOARD FOR UNIQUE HOMEWORK

If, for example, the concept of time-sequence was under consideration, homemade transparencies with overlays might show the growth of a bean from seed to fully grown plant, or the changes taking place in an apple tree throughout the four seasons. Show the children how to make transparencies! (See page 158)

PROVIDE A STORAGE AREA FOR COMPLETED
EXPERIMENTS AND PROJECTS

Use the top of the wardrobe closet. It is a good out-of-the-way place.

PROVIDE A STORAGE AREA FOR SCIENCE EQUIPMENT

Use a closet, a locker, an upended wooden orange crate, a spare book case. Have materials boxed, bagged, labeled, and have an inventory posted so that children may request and borrow.

Participating in a science fair

All these activities, these finding-out experiences, these field trips and experiments, these home projects and unique homework developments, lead painlessly, at the end of the year, to the science fair.

If, however, it so happens that your room is not overflowing with science projects, then you might want to use the *idea* of a science fair, to boost interest in science, and give it direction.

Show your children pictures of previous science fairs that had been held in your school. Show them pictures of national fairs. You'll find such pictures in the *Scientific American Magazine* and in *Science News*. Take your class on behind-the-scenes trips to the nearest Museum of Natural History, the Botanical Gardens, the Zoo. Not only will they see scientific work in progress, behind the scenes, they will also have opportunities to ask questions of *real* scientists.

If then, you have to prepare for a science fair, it will be easier for you to settle on one large topic. Talk it over with your class before making a decision. Fill the room with books and magazines keyed to the subject. After you've saturated the class with materials, you will be able to break the large topic down into workable projects.

Now you must decide on a calendar, and safety rules come next. Set up the safety rules and do not deviate from them. Make sure your children know they will *not* be permitted to use:

- Glassware, because it's breakable. Use plastic materials, instead.
- Combustible or other hazardous chemicals. They're dangerous.
- Cartridges containing solid, liquid or gaseous propellants.
- Electrical circuits requiring plug-in 110 volt lines. They are to use only battery hook-ups.
- Open flames of any kind.

What about the criteria for setting up and judging the exhibits? You need these criteria as much as your children do, so think along these lines:

- Every exhibit should show a scientific principle, e.g., plants need water to grow.
- It should be the answer to a problem or a question, e.g.: Aim—*to find out* if plants need water in order to grow. It should *not* be a demonstration of something already learned, so the aim should *not* read: To show that plants need water in order to grow.
- It should have clear labels.
- It should show a minimum of adult help.
- It should relate to the course of study of the grade, or it may illustrate an unusual problem that happens to be newsworthy.
- It should show originality and initiative. Collections and diagrams, in and of themselves, mean little.
- It should be within the child's comprehension.
- It should be three dimensional, with pertinent background material such as charts, reports, records, all clearly printed.
- It should be displayed or arranged in a box or on a board that is no less than 18″ by 24″.
- It should be dynamic, with moveable parts, if possible (and ringing bells and flashing lights).

When *the* day arrives, be a showman. Have a rexographed program ready which looks like this:

SCIENCE FAIR OF CLASS

Exhibitors	Title of Exhibit	Scientific Principle
1. Mary A.	Checking on a steady hand	A battery circuit may be used to detect changes in equilibrium.
2. Leon J.	Fuses protect against fire	Fuses have a low melting point.
3. Joan B.	About water	Surface tension can let a razor blade float in water.

- Get every child's name in print, if possible.
- Let every exhibitor wear a badge.
- Invite the parents.
- Be sure every exhibitor can explain his exhibit in a scientific manner.
- Be generous with praise and the children will work!

And after the class fair? No doubt your school will run a large scale science fair, and this means that your children will have a second chance to exhibit and explain.

Science is to find out—so take stock

The end of the term is coming up fast. Time to take stock. Besides acquitting themselves favorably on quizzes, book reports and occasional "papers," your children, in this age of science, have learned some of the ways of science.

They have learned how to prepare for and profit from trips; how to collect neighborhood plants and animals as well as non-living things; how to identify and prepare them for exhibits.

They have learned the six basic steps inherent in the scientific method of investigation, and are able to embark on finding out. Young children can complete projects and write them up on experience charts. Older children can record their work in their personal science notebooks.

Your children, under your guidance, have also learned that textbooks are for study and reference and stimulation. They have learned that films and filmstrips are especially valuable when getting started on a new topic or reviewing an old one. And they have become acquainted with the biographies of many of the great men and women of science.

Enthusiasm runs high. The children work like scientists, orderly and organized in their thinking and in their procedure. They even talk like scientists, using a precise scientific vocabulary from *A* to *Z*, from *aa*, a type of lava, to *zymolysis*, a chemical reaction that occurs in digestion. So much learning has taken place in your science section this year!

Are you sure?

Are you sure that you are not misinterpreting enthusiasm for solid learning in depth?

Learning in depth

Because science is considered a minor subject in the elementary schools, you will find it difficult to check on your children's learnings by way of standard tests. There are, however, ways of gauging learning in science, and one of these ways concerns *growth* in the kind of questions children ask.

Very little children ask, "What's that? And that?" Older ones ask, "What's that for? And what does it do?" With growth in understanding comes the *how* and *why*, the *suppose* and *if*.

To gauge growth in questioning ability, give the class a topic and ask each child to make up ten good questions.

Rate each question ten. How many 100's do you think you'll see?

Another way of gauging learning-in-depth in science is to observe the ways in which children handle the *answers* to their questions.

* Are they satisfied with flat statements?
* Do they challenge any answers?
* Do they retest any answers?
* Do they use these answers as stepping stones to finding out answers to deeper and more involved questions?
* What's their attitude toward scientific authority?
* Do they know the difference between scientific authority and TV commercials?

Watch your children in this respect. Get a lesson going, then sit by with a tally sheet. Place a check mark next to each child's name as he asks a question or volunteers an answer. This will give you an indication of the spread of the questions and answers in your class. You will quickly see who monopolizes the discussion and who withdraws from it.

Another time, use a tape recorder. Then you and your children, at a later date, can consider the quality of the questions and answers.

The kind of questions your children ask, the ways in which they satisfy their curiosity, and what they do with the answers, are all marks of their growth, as well as of their interest in science.

But the 30 new textbooks and the 30 new workbooks which you requested some time ago, *could not of themselves* have fanned this interest or sparked this development in a disinterested class.

7

Using the Multi-Media
for Increased Learning

Knowledge has doubled in the last decade. It will double again in the next. There is so much to be taught, and the days are just too short for this kind of escalated instruction. In addition, widespread mobility aggravates the situation. In a world of migratory workers, trailer camps and crowded cities, not too many teachers and children stay in any one place long enough to dig in. Such teachers are likely to be unfamiliar with the deep-seated aspirations of the community. Such children are likely to have acquired little in the way of sequential learning. Small wonder that teachers and children sometimes miss out on the satisfactions that go with a job well done.

Caught up by a sense of urgency, teachers tap each other for solutions, even in the lunchroom:

Does anybody get the daily plan completed? I never have enough time. . . . My children won't read anything but comics. . . . I made every child get a library card. . . . I always prided myself on my English. Now, I can't seem to communicate with my children. . . . Communicate? That's out! You can't reach these kids! . . .Then there is no solution?

There is a solution, and it's exactly right for this day and age. It works for big business; it will work for you. When business tycoons have soap to sell, they go on the air. They use the multi-media for audience involvement. They capture attention, they communicate effectively, and the soap sells.

You have learning to sell. So borrow the communication techniques of Madison Avenue, and use the multi-media like a precision tool. Then you will communicate effectively. Then you will reach your children. They will learn competently, and your time will be sufficient for escalated instruction.

With the multi-media, you immediately attract the attention of your children:

A picture catches the eye. . . . A recording evokes rhythmic responses. . . . A statue invites touching. . . . A rose induces sniffing. . . . A pot of bubbling chocolate stimulates the salivary glands.

But, like the pitchman on commercial television, you've got to do more than capture attention. You've got to follow through. This follow-through is, in essence, a design for teaching that is composed of six teaching steps; activated by four learning principles; and communicated by way of the audio-visuals: words and music, people, pictures and things.

This teaching design works so well that big business thinks nothing of spending $30,000 for a brief TV commercial that goes something like this:

Design for teaching—at $30,000 a minute

WITH SIX TEACHING STEPS

1. *Aim:* The aim is to sell soap, and the cast will, accordingly, be multi-racial.

2. *Motivation:* The scene opens with a strong motivation, slanted to appeal to the senses: There is background music, "Rock-a-Bye-Baby." There's an alluring

young woman wearing a diaphanous gown. There's a couch for reclining and flowers for enjoying, and a bassinet in the corner for an emotional hook.

The camera dollies in for a close shot of the rings on her left hand and the bar of soap in her right. The lettering, BLISS SOAP is clearly visible on the soap. "Hello, I'm a BLISS girl, and I have fragrant, inexpensive BLISS to thank for my beautiful life," and soap in hand, she dances around to the fireplace and picks up *his* picture. "Ah, BLISS—Take it from me, girls, BLISS MAKES YOU A PRINCESS!"

3. Presentation and Development: Cut now, to a Hollywood salesman for the presentation of facts. He develops, by way of object demonstrations, the merits of BLISS Soap: its beauty power, staying power, soothing power and emotional appeal. "It even shines diamond rings," he advises us gallantly.

4. Comparison: And for a comparison of BLISS with Brand X, he demonstrates differences in weights and ingredients.

5. Summary: Dissolve to the starry-eyed girl as she confidently recapitulates the merits of BLISS Soap as a personal experience.

6. Assignment: And now, for the homework, without which no lesson is complete. "Get BLISS," Mr. H. tells us. "BLISS! Three bars of BLISS only 77¢ at your neighborhood stores. Get beautiful! Get BLISS! Get in step with the BLISS Girl, for BLISS MAKES YOU A PRINCESS!"

And now, to the tune of "Rock-a-Bye-Baby," the BLISS Girl reviews the commercial:

Soap up with beauty,
Lather with BLISS;

BLISS brings romance to
Missus and Miss.

BLISS makes you fragrant
At work or play;
BLISS MAKES YOU A PRINCESS!
Get BLISS today!

Fade out . . . .

The public gets the message. BLISS gets the sales. And you get a $30,000 lesson capsuled into a 60-second commercial.

Now let's take this $30,000 lesson apart. Let's see what makes it so effective that one minute a day on television results in such vast public learning that BLISS sales zoom, and BLISS stock splits.

If only this kind of learning happened in the classroom! It will, if you activate your six-point teaching plan with these four learning principles:

WITH FOUR LEARNING PRINCIPLES

In the BLISS commercial, four principles of learning were directed at the viewer, personally and realistically. These were the principles of:

1. *Readiness.* Every woman is ready to get and/or keep the good things in life. BLISS shows her how.

2. *Varied Repetition:* This works best when the message is slanted to appeal to the senses, something the multi-media can do very well. In this brief run-down the word BLISS is repeated about 20 times: in print, in spoken words, in simple musical doggerel. It is repeated by an attractive male. It is repeated by an alluring female. It is repeated as a pleasing slogan, BLISS MAKES YOU A PRINCESS.

3. *One-Thing-at-a-Time:* The one thing emphasized throughout is the selling of BLISS Soap, and so, behind

the noisy and calculated hoopla, every word, every scene, every sequence, moves the viewer closer to buying the message and buying the soap. No distractions of any kind are permitted, not distracting words, nor activities, nor suggestions of any kind. (How many classrooms can boast of such tightly planned lessons without idle distractions!)

4. *Incorporation:* Learning is not completed until it has been incorporated into one's way of life. The viewer, having been exposed to the BLISS lesson, is directed to go out and buy. This is the homework assignment, and it completes the learning act.

These principles aren't new. They were practiced by Socrates and Aristotle, by Horace Mann and Montessori. They were practiced by your teachers, and they are practiced by you. What *is* new is the pace of implementation. Today's professional keeps one eye on capsuled time-teaching, and the other eye on the proliferation of learning.

So—let's put a classroom lesson together, using these same TV techniques: the six-point teaching plan, the four learning principles, and the audio-visuals. And lets develop this lesson at no extra cost to your board of education.

Design for classroom teaching

WITH REALIA

Take a routine bit of knowledge, something required in the primary grades—the sound of initial *B*. Use only the simplest form of the media, the "realia," the real things in your room. And plan precisely.

1. The aim? To teach children to recognize the sound of initial *B*.

2. Motivation? Since the children already know the alphabet by rote and can even sing it, declare this a

B Day because you have *Boys* in the room and you notice that the girls are wearing many *B* things!

3. For the presentation and development, use many and varied experiences involving the sound of initial *B*, and provide opportunities for repetition that will stretch the mind. Look around the room for realia, and:

> Call one boy and one girl to the front and ask the class to observe carefully the *B* things that are to be seen. Although the children can not yet read to any extent, print the words they suggest on the chalkboard. Your list will include: *boy* and *belt*, *buckle* and *beads*, and *bracelets*, *blue eyes*, *blonde* or *brown* or *black* hair, *big* ears, *biting* teeth, *braces*, *barrettes*— and more, if you ask the boys to empty their pockets!
>
> Now ask the children to look around the room for *B* things that they use. Collect these things as the children call them, and you will have a temporary exhibit on your desk. They will suggest *books* and *bells* and *balls*, *bags* of cookies, *boxes* of crayons, *Band-Aids*, *biscuits*, *bus* tickets, *book bags*, *briefcases* and *boots*.

4. For comparison play a *B* and no-*B* game. Ask the children to listen as they sit with their hands folded on their desks. If the word you call begins with a *B*, they are to raise one finger. If it begins with any other sound, they are to raise two fingers.

You will immediately be able to see the spread of learning or no-learning that has taken place with reference to the sound of initial *B*. If you need to back up and reenforce, you will.

5. To summarize, return to your list of *B* words on the chalkboard. Can the children draw appropriate pictures next to any of these words? They can and they do, as

you read a selected four or five. Now teach the class that this picture writing is called *rebus writing*; and explain that Primitive Man used rebus writing frequently. (It will help the lesson along if you have prepared yourself with a suitable book or picture about rebus writing, and can show it to the class at this time). Now—do the children think they can do some rebus writing at home about *B*'s?

6. The assignment grows naturally and enthusiastically out of the lesson, and the children are asked to bring in a rebus list of all the *B* things around their homes. The girls are to list *B* things inside their houses. The boys are to list *B* things outside their houses.

Whereas the TV commercial you are trying to emulate ended with one narrow learning directive, BUY BLISS, your lesson ends with an assignment which is a springboard for further learning. Note that the children, after bringing in their rebus list of *B* things, can be asked to bring in real *B* things and pictures. Then you are ready to set up a study display. Here, you will post *B* pictures on the rear board, and display the real things on the table below. With strings and properly lettered word cards, you highlight the growing vocabulary list. And, looking at it with your children, it's an easy step to the observation and notation of *categories* of *B* things: toys and animals, and games and good things to eat.

Such an important sound, this sound of initial *B!* It's important enough for booklets! So you make booklets and the learning continues. Each child makes his own, in any category he chooses, and you soon have *B* Animal Books, *B* Game Books, and *B* Doing Books (about bouncing and banging and bumping and barking). They will use pictures and drawings and rebus writing in their booklets, and may even paste in bits of real things.

And this adds up to a lot of learning for little children.

For a slam bang ending to this learning activity, develop

a big class book about *B* with your children. Of course, you will have to print it, but your children will illustrate it, and it could go something like this:

B is for *bicycle*
B is for *bear*
A teddy-bear bear
That sits in my chair!

B is for *barrel*, for *box* and for *bin*
B is for *basket* to keep my toys in!

Or you could develop a Riddle B Book that goes like this:

What sails on the ocean
And rhymes with a coat?
It starts with a *B*
It's called a big B_____!

When you are sleepy
You are a sleepy head,
Then it's time to take a B_____
'Cause it's time for B_____.

Now, was there ever such a sound as the sound of initial *B!*

Tune in next week, for the sound of final *B*—and the week after that, for the sound of middle *B!*

Unlike the TV commercial, this was a lesson (it was in fact a series of lessons) that cost nothing in the way of media materiel. Yet, it resulted in a great deal of learning, and that was because the children learned by direct experience with *real* things—with realia, a form of the multi-media. After that, the transfer to pictures and abstractions was a simple matter.

AND WITH WORDS

But direct experience with real things is not always possible. How, for example, can children experience the reality of something that happened long ago or far away?

"I'll tell my children about that," you say, but *telling isn't teaching.* If you try teaching only with words, even with printed words, you have no way of knowing how your children will translate those words. Remember that today's mobile children come to you with different linguistic levels, different social values, and different referent backgrounds. Try telling them a story, without showing them any pictures, and see what happens.

Tell, or read, the story of "Little Red Riding Hood." Then ask your children why Little Red Riding Hood's grandmother needed a nightcap in bed.

The city child will say "to cover her rollers."

The north country child will say "to keep her head warm."

The Negro child will say "to flatten her hair."

Now ask them to draw a picture of grandmother with her nightcap in bed, and see what you get from the sophisticated suburban child.

Children's answers invariably reflect their referent backgrounds. Ask, for example, what it means to be decent.

One child will say A-O.K.; another, to be sufficiently clothed for visitors; a third, to be respectable; a fourth, to be a square.

You never know, if your teaching is of the verbal type, what goes on in the heads of your 30 students.

Still, you cannot always provide real learning experiences for your children. So you do the next best thing. You provide simulated experiences by way of selected audiovisuals.

When you teach with things and pictures and the whole spectrum of the multi-media, you're more likely to get your message across, no matter how long ago or far away the content of that message. With the multi-media, you cut the stranglehold of words for all your students. You offer enrichment to the academically bright ones. You open the door to learning to those who are *language poor.* This you can do, because with the multi-media you build a core of common understanding that provides the readiness so necessary for the particular learning of any lesson you may design.

The initial *B* lessons involved simple learnings in the field of knowledge. Simple learnings can well be satisfied with simple realia.

More sophisticated learnings require more sophisticated materials. There are three areas of more sophisticated learnings: concept development; skill acquisition and the understanding of processes; character guidance.

Concept development constitutes the highest form of learning. It also constitutes the highest form of teaching, because: you have to challenge your pupils to play with newly acquired knowledges in terms of cause-and-effect; you have to spark discussion and guide your pupils in reaching and verbalizing a self-made generalization.

And this is not easy. But your multi-media will provide a common core of readiness for this kind of discussion, and your six-point teaching design will see you through.

Here is how it can be done.

With the Multi-Media

Suppose you have a middle grade and your course of study calls for the *development of concepts* in conservation. Move away from the trite oversimplification of plant-a-tree-when-you-cut-a-tree. This is the way of the easy conscience, and there is no time for the easy conscience when whole biomes are vanishing from the face of the earth!

- You could consider the vanished biome of the buffaloes who died out when the buffalo grass was stripped off the prairies.
- You could consider the vanishing biome of fresh water fish in the streams because of chemical and thermal pollution from industrial plants.
- You could consider the vanishing biome of wildlife in

the marshlands, as the water is drained to make way for the sprawling cities.

For little children, however, such considerations could be alarming and at the same time quite meaningless, because they provide little opportunity for identification. That's because identification for children requires the consideration of other children. So begin your development of conservation concepts with a consideration of the vanishing biomes of other children—on remote tropical islands and in the frozen lands of the far north.

Suppose then, you develop a unit on Lapland, a still intact biome, but one that's about to vanish as the Lapp children learn about the outside world and are tempted to leave their homes.

You provide your children with reading materials and take them to the museum where they learn about the partnership between the Lapps and the reindeer. They understand that in Lapland interdependence between man and beast is a fact of life. But what concepts have the children formed after listening to and reading thousands of *words* about the Lapps?

Do they believe that the good reindeer are the conscious benefactors of the Lapps?

Do they believe that the smart Lapps have consciously contrived their civilization around one small animal species?

For concept development

You want to make certain that sentimental, sociological generalizations do not take root in the minds of your children. As a matter of fact, you want to make certain that they discover a sound sociological concept that will serve them for life—the concept that *the environment determines the life-style of a people.*

The first thing you do now is to check the multi-media which you requisitioned some time ago for just this purpose. No matter what you find in the media kit, you preview it with two questions in mind: What's in this for my children? How can I use this material so that it leads to a sound, self-made generalization or concept by the children?

Your kit may contain such things as:

* A filmclip on "The Lapp Child Goes to Boarding School"
* A sound filmstrip on "The Annual Fair"
* A picture folio on "The Yearly Round-Up and Taxes"
* A pre-recorded tape on "Sounds in the Long Night"
* A color film on "The Semi-Annual Migrations of the Reindeer"

You note that your kit contains five forms of media, and, never forgetting the principle of one-thing-at-a-time, you plan five lessons, each one centering around one of these media forms. You begin each lesson with the same provocative challenges, a question that will rock your children and glue their eyes and ears to the media. You ask:

Is this partnership between the reindeer and the Lapps a 50-50 partnership? If it isn't: Is the reindeer the master? Is the Lapp the master? How do you know? Back up your opinion with *facts!*

With so provocative a challenge for viewing and listening, your children will become more than receptive consumers of the media. They will become active participants. They will ask to have bits and pieces played over. They will raise questions and objections, criticize the narrator's point of view, and call for point by point verification of facts. And you, having carefully previewed the material, will be ready to guide the kind of skillful discussion that leads to concept development. (See pp. 236 for discussion procedures.)

In the filmclip which runs about three or four minutes, your class will see Lapp children attending small, central boarding schools in the winter, when they are not needed to help with the reindeer migrations. In addition to reading and writing, the boys learn to carve reindeer horns and make skiis, the girls learn to cure skins and sew clothing. And all play lots of reindeer-oriented games. A girl holding a pair of antlers is "It" in a game of tag. A boy, running with antlers fastened to his head, is lassoed in a game of catch. A group playing a numbers game is using buttons made of reindeer bone. Are the Lapp children the masters because they play reindeer games? Are the reindeer the masters because they furnish the antlers and the bones?

In the same way, the other items in the multi-media kit may be considered, one a day.

In the sound filmstrip, the class sees reindeer products bartered at the annual fair for foreign necessities: salt and sugar, coffee, steel needles and an occasional hand-operated sewing machine. Whatever wealth the Lapps possess seems to stem from the reindeer. The reindeer never accumulate any wealth stemming from the Lapps. Who is master, here?

"The Yearly Round-Up of Reindeer and Taxes" is clearly pictured in the folio. There's no mistaking the fact that the government measures a Lapp's wealth by the size of his herd, and accordingly orders an annual round-up for the purpose of collecting taxes on the spot. It does indeed look as though it might indeed be the reindeer, the symbol of wealth, who is master in Lapland.

It would seem there'd be little to learn from the pre-recorded "Sounds in the Long Night of Lapland," but listen. You hear the rattle of ice pellets against the wooden cabin walls, the sh-shush of the wind across the frozen plains. You hear the howling of wolves and the answering whine of the dogs, the sudden clanging bell of the lead reindeer, and the stampeding of many hoofs. You hear the hoarse shouts of men, the whistle of a knife in the air, and a wolf howl, cut in half.

What you've just listened to is a common episode in the

long night, when Laplanders take turns standing sentry duty because the wolves are out and the reindeer need protection. What! Are the Lapps in the *service* of the reindeer?

You've now utilized four of the multi-media and there's one to go. As you turn to the film on the semi-annual migrations, your children inform you that they know all about the great spring drive, north to the mountain meadows, and the autumn drive, back south.

In the film, however, they see two or three sunny days signaling the end of winter. They see the reindeer growing restless, and in a wild, headlong movement, lighting out for the far north. Behind the deer hurry the Lapps, belongings strapped to the pack deer, babies in sleds behind the harness deer. Dogs bark, skiis fly, and the whole family races after the deer at 50 miles a day!

And this serves to strengthen some children in their opinion that the deer are the masters, for aren't the Lapps running after them? Almost like slaves!

This is the time to jolt the discussion with two questions that should crystallize the thinking in terms of conceptualization.

How do the reindeer *know* it's time to start on that northward migration? Are there any secret signs that tell them *this* is the day, and *this* is the hour? What can the reason be for this sudden movement to cooler, drier places?

Yes, the children will have to see portions of this film a second and perhaps a third time. You tell them the answers are there as clear as can be. They have only to look with their inner eye, and they have to make the most of what they see. They will have to make inferences. They will have to put two and two together.

And they do. They view the film again, and this time, they notice that the two or three sunny days melted the snow and softened the ground. They see that the softened ground turned muddy under the busy hoofs of the reindeer.

They see that the moss which grows on the frozen ground, became muddy and unfit to eat.

They infer that without moss to eat, the reindeer became hungry, and that hunger made them restless.

And then they see another sunny day and a swarm of insects! Of course. Gadflies and mosquitoes generally hatch during warm and sunny weather—another inference! Wouldn't you run if you were attacked by thousands of insects?

So the secret is a secret no longer. The reindeer are hungry. They are tormented by insects. They are stung into flight.

And this happens every spring, after sunny days trigger the migration to the north. It happens again every fall, when heavy rains trigger the migration to the south.

But you are still not ready to terminate this unit because the *children* have not yet developed the concept that *the environment determines the life-style of a people*—but you're close.

Any questions? Comments?

And yes, there are.

Child #1: When the reindeer run away from the mud, the vanished food, and the insects, aren't they just running away from bad living conditions?

Child #2: I think the Lapps are just looking after their property when they run after the reindeer. That makes the Lapps the masters, after all.

Child #3: Masters and slaves have nothing to do with it. It's the living conditions that make everybody run.

And now, with the one word *environment*, you are ready to wrap it up. You write it on the board. You explain that *environment* is the grown-up word for all-around-living-conditions.

"What makes a good environment for the Lapps?" you ask. And now, the children know:

* Reindeer make the environment good for the Lapps.
* Moss makes the environment good for the reindeer.
* Frozen ground makes the environment good for the moss.

"Then there are no slaves or masters in Lapland?"

There are no slaves or masters to make life good or bad. And the children tell you that it's the environment that makes life possible or impossible in Lapland.

And now you have the privilege of polishing this child-made generalization into the formal concept that the environment determines the life style of a people.

Once children develop a concept themselves, they can, with a little guidance from you, use this concept as a learning tool over and over again in their social studies. Put this concept to work the next time you take up the study of another simple community. Ask—How does the environment determine the life style of the people in:

a fishing village—and then what happens to the life style if atomic plants are built nearby?

a desert—and then what happens to the life style if dams and power plants are constructed there?

a forest—and then what happens to the life style if huge lumbering operations move in?

Older children can play with this same concept in terms of the more complex living conditions in the large cities. But make it easy for your children to back up their thinking with facts. Provide them with wisely selected multi-media.

It may not be easy to obtain all such pertinent teaching aids. Some school districts are rich in their multi-media inventories, others are not. If, however, you plan in advance, you will find that all sorts of wonderful audio-visual aids are yours for the asking. For free loans, try the local public libraries and the larger county systems. Try also the museums in the nearest towns. And for other leads, check the free materials catalogues in your principal's office and look through the popular teacher's magazines.

So far, we have considered the multi-media as a learning booster only in two areas of teaching and learning: in the imparting of knowledge, as in the initial *B* lessons; in the development of a concept as in the unit on Lapland.

It's in the area of skills and processes, however, that the multi-media is a learning booster without compare.

For skills instruction

Education is more than the acquisition of knowledges and the development of concepts. Occasionally, you have to power your children with assorted skills. Some are simple. Some are maddening:

- How do you thread a sewing machine?
- How do you throw a curved ball?
- How do you change from manuscript to cursive writing?
- How do you organize a notebook?
- How do you hyphenate words at the end of a line?
- How do you show perspective?

Assuming that you know how to do these things, your demonstrations will not always take with every child—certainly not with the absent child, nor with the child admitted to your class the day after your demonstration. With *film loops*, however, every child has a better chance to learn or to reinforce a given skill.

A film loop explains and demonstrates one particular skill in about two minutes. It will run and rerun by itself as long as needed, three times, four times or more, until it is turned off by the viewer. Designed for individual or small group use, a film loop may be referred to as often as necessary. It is always accurate, always available, always the same.

You will find the going easier if you use the right media for the right problem. Other than taking an actual field trip, what better way is there for children to learn about the process of dairying, bread baking, or steel making than to see it on film?

And it isn't always necessary to get the media, ready-made. Do you wish to develop a lesson on the seasons? Use transparencies and do it in terms of a cherry tree! Take a few sheets of acetate and some colored pencils, and show your bare tree in winter, on the static. Prepare overlay #1 to show some leaves and blossoms because it's springtime. Prepare overlay #2 to show additional leaves (more or less covering the blossoms) and cherries just barely red because it's summer. Prepare overlay #3 to show a boy in the branches that are laden with red cherries. Show a basket tied to him. (And you know it's fall!)

Use transparencies in a dozen different ways. Better still, help children learn how to make their own transparencies to show how to set the table for morning milk and cookies; how to cross the street, safely; how to paste a picture in a notebook.

For character guidance

No matter how much little children may learn in school, how sound their concepts, how expert their skills, there are those in every era who claim that *this* generation and *these* children lack character. If you are over 30, you're fairly certain it's so. If you are over 40, you're convinced. Nobody knows how effective the school can be in guiding character. Certainly our efforts in this area will not hurt anyone. They may even open doors to visions of heroic splendor and world empathy.

For character guidance, then, use films for re-creating the lives of great men and great women of all races. Use recordings to bring to life the stirring speeches of bygone leaders. Use flat pictures, copies of old lithographs and steel engravings to light up the authentic past.

And for the character guidance of very little children, use short, one-reel films on habit formation on: "How to Get Ready for School," "How to Make Friends," "How to Behave when Visiting."

It would be a good idea to remember that films and recordings, pictures and realia are not substitutes for you and your six-point teaching plan. Even though today's children are media minded and have trained themselves in the all-at-onceness of TV projection, they need your help if they are to read the media to best advantage.

It would also be a good idea to remember that children want to learn and they want learning to happen fast. So: (1) don't hamstring them with words; (2) don't spoonfeed them with workbooks; (3) don't hold them back.

Try communicating with them in the tempo of today.

And then your days will be long enough, and you will complete *more* work than you ever thought to indicate in your daily plan!

8

Motivating for Mastery in Math

Do you believe the teaching of math will soon become obsolete because gas pumps are automatic, cash registers make change, and accountants check out our tax returns?

Are you convinced that math is OUT because computers are IN?

Would you say that math is nobody's business?

Forget it. Math is everybody's business!

Consider your personal involvement in math. You have a bank account, a pension plan and credit cards. You're insured to the hilt against contingencies. Daily, you note the astronomical spending planks in the political platforms. You are familiar with the governor's bulging budget. Excellent! Are you equally well informed as to the effect this spending will have on your standard of living in the next decade? Do you know what probabilities circumscribe your statistical entity in today's world?

It's true that much of the world's business and the calculations of science are run through computers. That's because computers can add, subtract, multiply, divide and make predictions with unbelievable speed. Computers are great for the mechanics of math. People are better for handling personal and environmental concerns. And this includes children.

Two steps in motivating children

If your children are unmoved by the school's standard offerings in math, you can soon change that. You can motivate them in two steps. You ask them to begin with the math that surrounded them the day they were born.

STEP #1—HOW TO RECONSTRUCT A MATHEMATICAL FIRST DAY ON PLANET #3

A challenging assignment titled "Mathematics and My First Day on Planet #3" will quickly involve every child and his parents in an overwhelming clutter of mathematical facts. The title alone starts off with two such facts. Can the children come up with ten or twenty? A hundred shouldn't surprise you. Try it with your class and see:

Janie was born—when? What day? What month? Year? Hour?

What was she like? Doctors check by counting: how many eyes? Ears? Nostrils? Arms? Fingers and toes?

What were her measurements? Length and weight?

What was her blood pressure? Pulse rate? Temperature? (Her baby chart will contain all this information.)

And what formula was prescribed for her? How many ounces of milk and water? How many teaspoonsful of sugar? How many minutes required for boiling at 212 degrees F.?

Other mathematical data might include the address of the hospital, the doctor's fee, the size of her bassinet.

So started, Janie's list could go on to include mathematical descriptions of relatives who visited her, the number and value of the gifts they brought, as well as meteorological data from the back records of the Weather Bureau.

What to do with this flood of mathematical data when the children bring in their completed assignments? Post it all on the bulletin board. And what to do with the children's unleashed and, by now, competitive enthusiasm? Channel it!

Channel it by showing them how to develop a *Time Line*, and you will be on Step #2 in your drive to motivate interest in math.

STEP #2—HOW TO MAKE UP A TIME LINE THAT BECOMES AN AUTOBIOGRAPHY IN MATH

No child will be able to resist making up his mathematical autobiography, which is what his Time Line will turn out to be. And this is the way to do it.

Provide each member of your class with a large sheet of newsprint. If the age range in your class is from nine to ten, show all the children how to fold the paper into 12 equal columns. The first column, set off by a double line, will indicate a partial listing of mathematical involvements. The last column, also set off by a double line, will leave room for predictions. The ten columns between, will represent ten years and the chart, at the beginning, will look like this:

Let the children use the largest sheets of newsprint you can obtain, so they will have room for pictures, snapshots and small items of memorabilia, as well as for numerical notations. At this time, however, collect these skeletal, unfinished charts, and store them, while the children develop their collection of facts in their notebooks and folders. Allow three days for this collection, because the children will be finding mountains of mathematical data about themselves as they interview parents, neighbors, friends, relatives and community workers, revealing a tremendous amount of self-motivation, drive, mathematical calculation and discovery.

The children will be fascinated by the diversity of measurements pertaining to themselves:

Claudia—that at age 10, she is 59 inches tall, weighs 112 pounds, wears a size 11 dress, an 8 coat, a 20 hat, 6½ in gloves, 5C in shoes, and a 9 in stretch socks!

Jerry, a great eater—that he consumes almost a ton of food a year.

Janie's Mathematical Time Line

Class _____   Born _____

	1st yr.	2nd yr.	3rd yr.	4th yr.	5th yr.	6th yr.	7th yr.	8th yr.	9th yr.	10th yr.	Predictions
My Math Environment											
Personal Facts											
Health											
Growth											
Clothing											
Other											
Family Facts											
Other Facts											

Alex—that he breathes 15,000 quarts of air a day, and uses 20 gallons of hot water for a shower.

Some children will note allowances, earnings, expenditures, savings and curfews. Others will note the license numbers of their family cars, and the serial numbers on their dollar bills.

Transferring all this data to their charts will become so important an activity you will want to make sure the children do justice to themselves. This means that you will need to supervise them carefully according to previously agreed upon standards of arrangement.

When all the Time Line Charts are completed, hang them on the walls. They are remarkable. Unbelievable. Startling. Proof positive that your children's interest in math is boundless.

Pause a moment. You've stirred up a mathematical storm. Why did you do it?

Because you believe that such high level motivation is the mark of a creative teacher? (That's true.)

Because you believe that the ability to engage children in such organized experiences is the mark of an organized teacher? (That's true, too, and there's even the touch of a pro here.)

Because you believed that each of these carefully prepared Time Lines would be evidence of mathematical power in your children, and that your math worries for the year would be over? *Not true!* It is evidence only of the fact that you have motivated your children most professionally, to the point where they are eager and willing to engage in math activities. Mathematical power is still to be developed. This means that you have still to equip them with mathematical prowess, meaning mathematical understandings and concepts and skills and knowledges.

But what mathematical concepts and skills and knowledges you are responsible for with reference to your particular children and your particular grade—that is the question.

The answer to this question is a plan, a plan that will help you implement the interest you've released in terms of your mandated responsibilities.

Implementing motivated interest in math

This brings you to a professional planning plateau, and on this plateau you lay out your *long range* plans for the required work of the year, and the *short range* plans for the daily and weekly activities.

This is a big job. How you go about it will determine the kind of teacher you will become. Plan with heart and mind and imagination, and you will become a great teacher. Plan casually, indifferently or impulsively, and the shining rewards of teaching will pass you by. The job of sound planning is time-consuming and hard, but then—nobody ever said that teaching was easy!

So, here are some suggestions that will make the job of planning a little easier.

PLANNING THE REQUIRED WORK FOR THE YEAR WITH A LONG RANGE PLAN

Take a hard look at the topics that interest your children, and take a harder look at the topics that are mandated.

Make no mistake about the importance of the mandated work because that is what you are employed to teach, as creatively, as imaginatively and as thoroughly as you can. So:

Familiarize yourself with the topics in your course of study and check out those topics in your textbooks. Review the course of study of the grade below so you know what you have to build on. Review the course of study of the grade above so you know what you are supposed to build toward.

Then, aware of the learnings you are responsible for, and aware of the fact that you have only ten months in which to develop these learnings with your motivated class, you lay out a "Projected Time Line for Teacher," on a skeletal form, something like this:

GRADE

Teacher's Projected Time Line of Work

	Sept.	Oct.	Nov.	Dec.	Jan.	Feb.	Mar.	April	May	June
Mandated Topics New for the grade										
References										
Pages										
Old Topics Basic to Understanding the Above New Topics										
References										
Pages										
Materials Needed										
Provisions for:										
Reviews										
Testing										
Retesting										

Such a Projected Time Line will provide a preview of the required work for the year, and enable you to plan a solid program in math. But your children had other ideas, remember? So try these suggestions for spice and meaning. Include in this projected plan for the year, every possible topic of demonstrated class interest that you can tune in with the prescribed topics. Weave the children's other mathematical interests into other areas of the curriculum.

And this brings you back to the children's Time Lines that are posted all over the place. Altogether, the class seems to be interested in just about everything mathematical: from hi fi decibels to home run scores to light years. You are amazed by the hundreds of items, all important to them. Don't be. Utilize the skill of classification (see Chapter 6) and your program will begin to move.

With the help of the class, get those countless items off the Time Line Charts and onto your chalkboard. And then ask your children one question: *Which of these things seem to go together in terms of the way in which they are measured?* And the answer is obvious. These items may be measured according to weight, length, liquid volume, temperature, speed and time!

At this point, your children may volunteer to find out the names of the measuring instruments and to collect the instruments and bring them in for an exhibition. (And if they don't, you can always suggest that yourself!)

Inside half an hour, order will emerge from the chaos on your chalkboard, and you will now have a classified list that will look something like the table on p. 169.

Although this chart of measures and measuring devices is fabulous, it is also incomplete, as you know from referring to your course of study. So direct your children to their textbooks and reference materials to round out their observations and to complete the standard Tables of Measure. This is a job that could easily overwhelm them, so make light work of it. Involve everybody in committees and start them on the

WE MEASURE

#1 Some things by:	#2 In units of:	#3 With special equipment such as:
weight	ounces, pounds, tons, grams, etc.	scales (assorted kinds)
length (and distance)	inches, feet, yards, miles, kilometers, etc.	rulers, yardsticks, tape measures, transits, fathometers, odom-eters
liquid volume	cubic centimeters, quarts, etc.	standard measuring spoons, barrels, quarts, pints, gallons
speed	m.p.h. or r.p.m.	speedometers, anemometers
temperature	degrees, Fahrenheit degrees, Centigrade degrees, Celsius	thermometers (assorted kinds)
sound	decibels	audiometers
light	wave lengths	interferometers
pressure	inches millimeters	barometers sphygmomanometers
time	seconds, minutes, hours, days, years, etc.	clocks, watches, calendars, sundials, shadows, etc.

more common tables: Linear, Square and Cubic. Then ask
the committees to include in their reports the ways in which
these measures show up on their way to school. Within the
next day or two, assign other committees to work on Avoir-
dupois, Apothecaries, Liquid and Dry Measure, and top it
off with Circular and Paper Measures, reminding the children again, to indicate ways in which these measures crop
up in their daily lives at home and in school.

Now to wrap up this activity, tangibly.

Collect the committee reports and staple them into a
Classbook of Measures. Your children will draw immeasur-
able pride from this booklet. You, yourself, will refer to it
throughout the year, as the topic of measure and measurement comes up periodically in your overall plan.

But a long list of exciting mathematical topics that do
not fit into your overall plan still remains! If you leave these
topics out, your children will be let down. They are now
highly motivated in math, and that was what you wanted,
wasn't it?

Take advantage of this bubbling motivation by correlating math with social studies, science, and the language
arts!

* In social studies, include opportunities for your children to apply their mathematical ingenuity to map
  projections, to the plotting of distances on land and
  sea like navigators, and beneath the sea, like subma-
  rine commanders.
* In science, provide experiences that call for micro-
  measurements with reference to the size and number
  of bacteria, molecules and algae; and macromeasure-
  ments with reference to the problems of space and
  meteorology; and the measurement of more familiar
  things: wind speed and air pressure, humidity and
  the changing length of days.

- In language arts, involve your children in researching the lives of the great mathematicians; in developing their mathematical vocabulary and putting it together into a Math Dictionary.

And, with a little lighthearted resourcefulness, you can guide your children in correlating math with music and physical activities and art. Think about it!

Now pause a moment. You've involved your children in three sparkling activities: "My First Day of Life on Planet #3," "My Mathematical Time Line Autobiography," and "The Classbook of Measures." And, in so doing, you involved them in more mathematical experiences than the average teacher manages in a year!

Admittedly, these are upper grade experiences. But second and third graders have exactly the same interests! You have only to stay within the scope of their understanding, and they, too, will be able to grasp and apply some of the tables of measures in their every day observations. They, too, will be able to make maps (of the neighborhood), to weigh, measure and compare simple concrete items in science, and to develop a Classbook of Measures and a Primary Math Dictionary.

One of the most important things in mathematics, is to ignite interest by way of personal involvement. This you have done for your children. And for yourself, you've laid out a long range plan for the year. So far, it has been an exciting and worthwhile experience, but to make the year *rewarding* for yourself and your children, you now need to break down your long range plan into manageable, everyday activities. This means you have to know in advance what you are going to do every day of the week. And this brings you to short range planning in terms of weekly and daily plans. With such plans, you'll be able to develop each topic, step by step and in sequence, and to develop mastery in your children, step by step, for unbroken understanding.

PLANNING MANAGEABLE SHORT RANGE TEACHING
AND LEARNING ACTIVITIES

Here's a sketchy sort of outline that many teachers find
helpful when planning the week's work:

For the week of_____

*Aim*_____New work_____
                 Review work_____

*References*_____

    Texts: titles and pages
    Other references: titles and pages
    Course of study: pages

*Materials*_____

    Concrete
    Representational
    Audio-Visuals

Approach and Development

    Activities
    Experiences

Provision for

    Games
    Teasers
    Reinforcement
    Drill for immediate response
    Assignments

*Special Provisions for Individual Needs Re Knowledges,
Skills, Concepts*

Assorted Testing Techniques for Mastery
(See Chapter 11, p. 240)

Such an outline is, at best, a guide, in that it indicates
how much you hope to cover for the week. Keep it flexible

and flesh it out, day by day, as necessary. For fleshing out this guide, however, you will need some help.

Your best sources of help for this kind of precise planning are to be found in your textbooks and in the sample texts in your principal's office; in your teacher's guides and manuals; in your course of study; and for exciting, up to the minute ideas, in the filmstrips and trade books located in your school library. Here you will come across different approaches and different procedures necessary for reaching your different children.

Make these approaches and procedures your own, and you will soon be able to teach with such smooth continuity that your children's understanding will be clear, their grasp assured, and you will have no reason to backtrack, to reteach ad infinitum, or to engage in the foreverness of remedial work.

Here are two procedures that will help you do just that:

1. When presenting new material within a familiar topic, keep a sharp eye out for *gradations of difficulty*. This means, for example, that in your teaching of multiplication, you postpone the zero difficulty in a three-digit multiplier such as 302 or 320 until your children are thoroughly conversant with the algorism for multiplying by three digits.

It means that in the consideration of two-step problems, such as "If three items cost 30¢, how much for two dozen?" you build up to the second step by way of four easy levels and the necessary illustrative materials:

- Three items cost 30¢; how much will one cost?
- Three items cost 30¢; how much will six cost?
- Three items cost 30¢; how much will one dozen cost?
- Three items cost 30¢; how much will two dozen cost?

And in the same way, you tackle such problems as "If three items cost 50¢, how many can you get for $5?

2. When presenting a new topic, keep an equally sharp eye out for the sequential development between the old topic

174   MOTIVATING FOR MASTERY IN MATH

and the new, meaning, for example, that you first make sure
that your children understand fractions and the ways of fractions before you attempt to introduce the whole new topic
of decimals.

As long as you remain in the profession, your ability to
grade difficulties and to proceed sequentially will be syn-
onymous with your skill in the teaching of subject matter.

The skill of your children in learning this subject matter
is another thing altogether. On the one hand, they can learn
by way of rote memorization. This is instant learning, quick,
noticeable, and exact. Unfortunately, however, this kind of
learning is subject to equally quick and noticeable forgetting
unless it is kept in constant use. On the other hand, your
children can learn by way of power skills that will give direction to the utilization of their common sense. This is not
to say memorization is out. It is to say that those learning
skills that are systematically powered by correct and meaningful practice are hard to beat.

**Activating mathematical interest with learning
skills and concepts**

Of the many mathematical skills that will stand your
children in good stead, these two easy ones can make the
environment come alive at any grade level—the skill of precise nomenclature; the skill of estimating.

How to Apply the Skill
of Precise Nomenclature

The skill of precise nomenclature goes hand in hand
with precise mathematical thinking which is based on precise observation. Since you've involved your children in measurement, push ahead now in this same area and see what use
you can make of precise observation.

Just about everything you can see, and many things
that you cannot see, can be measured. And anything that
can be measured, from sound waves to skyscrapers, has some

kind of shape. Shapes found in nature are freeform and hard to measure. Shapes found in math, the geometric shapes, are precise in form, have precise names, and can be measured according to precise formulas.

There are many geometric shapes to be seen in your classroom, and this is something that children of any age are interested in. So look around—can the children find any flat or *plane* shapes? A square wall? A rectangular floor or desk top? A triangular tear in the window shade? A circular graph on the chalkboard? Good!

Now, can they find *solid* shapes? The globe?—Yes, a sphere! Your desk minus the legs?—A parallelepiped! The can of soda?—A cylinder! The small pyramid?—A tetrahedron! And the party hats in the closet?—Cones!

Make sure your children know the difference between plane shapes and solid shapes precisely, by checking them out with a few common "don't's":

* *Don't* call a ring a circle. Why not?
* *Don't* say a box is a square even if all six sides have exactly the same measurement. Why not?
* *Don't* say a wedge is a triangle. What is it, then?
* *Don't* say a penny is round and so is a ball. They should know the difference between a disc and a sphere!

Can your children list ten or twenty additional "don't's?" Of course, they can! Take these "don't's" with you when you go for a walk to look for more geometric shapes, and take along notebooks and pencils so that no shapes, plane or solid, get away from the children.

As you leave the building, do the children see the square plane shapes on the sidewalk? Do they see the cylindrical telephone poles (not precisely shaped, however) and the gas storage tanks and the garbage cans? Do they see the coiled garden hose? The flag flying on top of the metal flag pole? The advertising balloon overhead? What shapes? And what shapes do they see when they look at the houses and gas stations and bicycles and shop windows?

What your children do with the notations in their notebooks when they return to the classroom, depends, in part, on their ages.

If your children are very young, an exhibit, set up in the rear of the room, showing common solid shapes (the kind they saw on their walk) labelled and flanked with pictures of related plane shapes, would seem to be sufficient.

If your children are older, refer them to their texts for precise ways of determining the measurements of shapes.

And you will find it very exciting to acquaint your children with the three-way rule that applies to the creation of almost all standard architectural shapes from the Taj Mahal to the Empire State Building. This three-way rule calls for three precise words: *level, square,* and *plumb,* and they refer to three precise characteristics that have to be built into buildings if they are not to collapse: the floors must be level; the walls must be plumb, meaning vertical; and the corners have to be square, meaning 90-degree right angles. So provide yourself with three precision tools: a spirit level, a T square, and a plumb bob line which your school janitor is sure to have or can easily borrow for you, from the school carpenter.

Then take your class for another walk, to see a house that is under construction. With the permission of the carpenters, let your children use the spirit level and discover for themselves whether the floors are level. Let them use the plumb bob line, and check to see whether the walls are really plumb perpendicular to the floor. Let them use the T square and find out if the walls are at right angles to each other and to the floor and ceiling.

Back at school, they may discover some slight deviations when they check out your classroom with the level, plumb bob and T square. Such deviations are common because buildings "settle." If the deviations in your classroom are noticeable, especially if you find that the right angles are considerably off, start your children on measuring all sorts of angles—a most timely skill in these days of guided missiles and unmanned spaceships. And put this skill to work as you develop the geometric portion of your mathematics course of study.

Should you have a brilliant run-away class in math, challenge them with *projections* of shapes, a pastime that is dear to the hearts of professional mathematicians. And here's a favorite puzzler, calling for precise observation.

Choose a bright, sunny morning for this puzzler, and clear away the seats and desks beneath a southern window. Direct the children's attention to the shape of the window panes projected on the floor by the sun. Have the projection chalked out, and compare it with the window. Is the shape exactly the same? Are the angles the same? Is the size the same? No to all three questions! Well, is anything the same? And the answer is yes on two counts: in each instance, the sides are parallel, and there are four distinct corners on each of the panes as well as on the projection.

If, later in the afternoon, your children chalk in another projection of the window panes, the shapes will again be different in some ways, the same in others. The children will be able to see that the sides are still parallel, and that the four corners are still there—but what has happened to the corners? Set your brilliant class to find an explanation for that!

Whether you have older children or younger ones, bright, normal or slow, they will be convinced by this time that they're pretty good in measurement and quite expert in recognizing shapes and angles.

Are they?

Face them with a boxful of common items: a length of twine, a rubber band, a handful of granulated sugar in a plastic bag, a hard boiled egg, a beaten egg in a cup, a sharpened pencil, a soda straw, a few empty ice cream cones of assorted sizes, a quarter-pound bar of butter, and anything else you can think of.

Provide yourself with a ruler, a tape measure and a small scale, and as you remove the items from the box, ask the children to test their knowledge of measurements and shapes.

Start with the butter. The children say it's a parallelepiped? Splendid! Now suppose you cut dainty slices for serving purposes! The slices are square-shaped? Good. Suppose you place the butter dish on the warm radiator. What shape does the butter assume? Does the weight remain the same? Use the scales to find out!

What about the twine? And sugar? Shape and amount? You say you put a handful of sugar into the box. Would it make a difference if someone else's hand had been used? How would you measure the rubber band? As for the cones, would the biggest one hold twice as much as the smallest? How could you find out?

Again your children will bubble with enthusiasm. Excellent! This means they are ready for a lesson on *estimating* which is nothing more or less than the ability to make educated guesses, a most valuable asset in life.

How to Apply the Skill of Estimating

The ability to estimate depends on experience and common sense. So, if you'll supply the experience, your children will supply the common sense. What to do? Set up a lesson on estimating something that is available in the room.

Since many children bring lunch to school, check out the lunch sacks. Does anyone have apples, bananas, cookies? Good! Collect four apples, two bananas, half a dozen cookies, and a thermos of soup. Now clear your desk and place on it your scale (requisitioned from the supply room or brought from home or borrowed from the nearby grocer). Draw a chart on your chalkboard for educated guesses and it will look something like this:

Educated Guesses Concerning Weight

Items	Highest Estimate	Lowest Estimate	Actual Weight on Scale
Apples			
Bananas			
Cookies			
Thermos			

Now do the same for something that is common to the children—collect and weigh footgear, and your chart, depending on the season, will look something like this:

Educated Guesses Concerning Weight

Items	Highest Estimate	Lowest Estimate	Actual Weight on Scale
1 boy's sneaker			
1 girl's slipper			
1 moccasin			
1 ghillie shoe			
1 sandal			
1 overshoe			
1 boot			
1 stretch boot			

The guesses will range amazingly, and the estimates, compared with the actual weights, will astonish your children. Don't stop now. Provide some more experiences in estimating! Have them estimate linear measurements, temperature and time. Then have them do the actual measuring so they can check on their estimates.

Here are some simple activities that will lend themselves to estimating on almost every level:

- Divide the class into pairs of buddies. Have each child estimate the height of his partner and the size of his waist line. Then check, record, and marvel!
- Take three empty soda cans. Fill one with cold water from the tap. Fill one with cold water and ice cubes. Fill one with nothing. That is, leave it empty. Now have the children insert a forefinger into each of the cans and estimate its temperature. Then check the actual temperatures with thermometers.
- Provide yourself with a stop watch and explain to the children that here's a chance to estimate time. Let them sit quietly while you allow a minute to pass. Then ask them how long they think they sat there! If, after several such time exposures, they think they have a good idea of a minute, ask them what they can do in a minute:

How many times can they wiggle their thumbs in a minute? Get their estimates, then clock them.

How many times does their pulse beat in a minute? Estimate and check by counting and looking at a large face clock.

How far can they walk in a minute? A block? 2 blocks? Take them outdoors—ready, set, go, and check!

Such gay activities provide some very real learning, and carefully planned homework assignments will help your children stretch this learning. For homework, then, ask them to estimate:

How many pounds of hamburger would be needed for a family of five?

How many gallons of paint to paint their bedrooms?

How many yards of cloth to make a boy's sleeping bag?

How many sandwiches could they make out of one loaf of bread?

How many loaves of bread would be needed for a class picnic?

MOTIVATING FOR MASTERY IN MATH

Direct the children to check their estimates with such experts as mother and dad, the butcher and the painter. Ask them, too, to find out what is meant by an estimate that is given by building contractors. And assign committees to interview a carpenter, a mason, a painter, a plasterer and an electrician in order to find out three things:

—what is meant by an estimate in business;
—what an estimate includes;
—why some estimates are high and some are low for the same job.

When your children have learned to make estimates about real things that concern them, they will more easily learn how to estimate answers in straight numerical work. And this will serve as a good check on the sensibleness of answers to problems. Ask, for example:

If one hat costs $4.95, how would they estimate the bill for four hats?—$18.00, $20.00, $14.95?

If a trip ticket costs $1.10, how much, by estimation, would the bill be for the class of 25 children?—$25, $35, $250?

And what instant estimate would they come up with, if asked how much ice cream sodas would cost for the entire school of 983 children, if the sodas cost 25¢ each? $2500? $250? $25? Or $2.50?

So far so good, but the time has come to face the fact that you have fewer than 150 hours in which to nail down the required work in math. It is inconceivable that you and your class could continue to rocket along on such jet propelled and free wheeling motivation, to say nothing of the preparation demanded of you, just to keep one step ahead. True, your children have learned a couple of mathematical skills, but you need to implement these skills in some organized fashion and to move them along with some degree of systematic instruction.

Moving mathematical learning skills by way of systematic instruction

Keep that enthusiasm going, but don't bask in it. As you develop your number concepts, shape and direct your enthusiasm with three flanking operations: with the intelligent utilization of pertinent processes; with provision for frequent and correct practice; and with day by day pupil and teacher evaluation of every specific math learning which your lesson was supposed to further.

And you do this to the point of mastery! Nothing else will do if you are a teacher, and here is how to do it!

How to Develop a Number Concept, Systematically, in Four Easy Steps

To develop a number concept which means the comprehension and appreciation of a number, you build up to it by way of four steps: using *real* things and experiences; considering *pictures* of real things and experiences; moving into the use of *representational materials*, that is, materials that only represent real things, such as five chalk marks on the board to represent five children in the first row; and working with *numerals* which are abstractions for real things.

With upper grade children, you will be concerned with developing the concept of decimal numbers. With very young children, you will be concerned with numbers under ten. With somewhat older children, you will consider numbers above ten, for example the number 12, and then you will be developing not only the concept of this number, but also the concomitant process which is the bridging of tens.

Suppose it's 12 you wish to develop. Follow the four steps:

In Step 1, consider the *real* things and experiences that pertain to 12 because you want the children to appreciate the unique twelveness of 12. Bring in variously shaped egg cartons. Display double six packs of soda cans. Rearrange the seating plan in your room so you have six double tables on one side, and two rows of six single tables on the other side. Check out the birthdates of your children, write the 12 months horizontally on your board, and ask the children to arrange themselves accordingly.

The twelveness of 12 is not to be disputed! Even young children will volunteer information concerning other twelves: the 12 Apostles, the 12 Tribes of Israel, the 12 signs of the Zodiac, the 12 men on a jury, and of course, the clock with its 12 hours!

In Step 2, consider *pictures*. Not all will highlight the twelveness of 12. Some may show only 12 children in a ring, 12 oranges in a bin, 12 toys in a window, 12 disparate items in a lady's purse. All refer to and enrich the idea of 12.

In Step 3, you move into *representational materials*. You work with your magna board and magna discs, with your bead frames and beads, and encourage the children to arrange the discs and beads in assorted groupings totalling 12. You use pennies and encourage similar groupings. And lastly, you suggest to the children that they might be able to show 12 on the board, on their papers and in their homework books, by way of dots in various groupings.

In Step 4, you introduce the *numeral* 12 by writing it on the board. You review the idea of 12. You return to your 12 pennies and ask if there's another way of expressing this sum of money. And of course! Your children know that a dime and two pennies will do it!

Dramatize this answer by taping the dime and two pennies on a poster, and you are launched on the process of bridging tens (*Figure 9A*).

And now you have to teach your children that in math, a *ten* would represent a dime, and a *unit* would represent a penny. Then, utilizing this new information, relabel your poster so that it looks like Figure 9B.) And your children are

Figure 9A

only a breath away from catching on to the idea that in the numeral 12, the one refers to one *ten*, and the two refers to two units.

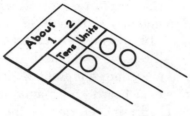

Figure 9B

    Such splendid lessons! How much your children are learning! You feel great! Professional! And you should. But if you want to keep on feeling like that, make sure this learning is "for real," and learning is only for real when it is used over and over, correctly and intelligently.

    To ensure such a state of affairs, make a practice of giving daily five-minute quizzes, either at the end of the lesson to find out if your children grasped the specifics you've just taught them, or at the beginning of next day's lesson as a warm-up indicator as to what needs clarification. And if your children are very young, check by way of number games! Also assign homework to reinforce that which needs to be reinforced, and to extend and enrich that which is understood. And you return to the many and various topics periodically in your daily five-minute check-ups so that forgetting doesn't get a chance to set in.

And, of course, you check and keep records. Better still, you let your records keep *you*—on your toes, so that all your hard work will not be in vain, and your children's learning will be "for real."

And the next chapter, "Making School Records Work for You," will show you how to do this.

9

Making School Records
Work for You

In today's mobile and complex culture, the facts of life are increasingly recorded on paper and tape, film and microfilm. No meteorologist can afford to ignore the recorded pattern of storm signals. No doctor can disregard a patient's medical history. No policeman can overlook the coded life style of a criminal suspect. And no broker can blind himself to the computerized credit rating of a client.

And yet, this is exactly what some teachers occasionally do when they think: "Records? When I teach, my children learn, and that's all that matters to me." . . . "I don't need records to tell me who's bright and who's dull." . . . "I can always tell what my children learned and what they haven't learned. *I* know!"

How can a teacher know such things? Would you, on receiving a shaky second grade, automatically know which children are reading on grade, above grade, below grade? Which are ready for the second grade speller, and which have not yet learned their 26 letters? Would you have in-

187

stant knowledge as to who is a whizz in science? Who has poor vision? Who is an occasional truant?

You can obtain this kind of information by giving diagnostic tests and being alert, but consider the time and labor involved! So go ahead, look at the record and see Who's Who in your class.

But look at the record with a critical eye. Although there's much that school records reveal, there's also much they conceal. They reveal statistical data that will help you organize your class. They conceal the truth, at times, by inadvertent inaccuracies, typographical errors, notations of personal bias, and omission of pertinent information. If you find discrepancies—check!

There are several categories of school records and, used judiciously, every one of them can make your work easier. Of these categories, the school's official records are permanent; the teacher's progress records are semi-permanent; the pupils' personal records are scratchy or elaborate, depending on their aims and your guidance.

Official records are fourfold in substance

These official records are cumulative cards, mandated and on-going. They follow the children from grade to grade, from school to school. They contain statistical data that each teacher in turn adds to, thereby keeping the record up to date. If you consider this a chore, you are not alone, but official records include four reserves of particulars that you cannot afford to overlook:

- the health record
- the attendance data
- behavior patterns
- scholastic achievement

Read these official records in September. An hour or two so spent will give you a working knowledge of the little problems that plague your children, and contain the makings of classroom distractions for you.

HEALTH RECORDS REVEAL PHYSICAL FITNESS FOR LEARNING

You look at the health cards and you note that: five children have poor vision and one suffers a hearing loss; five are well grown and above average in height; six are undersized and one has a weak bladder; two attend speech class; one occasionally falls asleep at his desk. Twenty-one casualties? No. These are simply physical variations within the group.

Three ways to accommodate physical variations in the classroom

You will help these children function normally if you take their physical variations into account. You do this by drawing up a temporary seating plan. You place the three with poor vision, up front and near the windows; the child with the hearing loss next to your desk where he can hear you; the lispers also next to your desk, for comfort; the child with the weak bladder, near the door, so he can leave when necessary. You arrange to see the nurse about your sleeper, and you still have to accommodate your very tall and very small children. For them, you may have to request furniture that fits, but you will take care of that after you have met your class and seen how much each one has grown over the summer.

ATTENDANCE RECORDS TELL A STORY

You may be a champion good teacher, but you *cannot teach an absent child.* So look at your attendance records. You will find some children whose attendance is spotty. And spotty attendance tells a story of overly permissive parents or casually indifferent parents; of a new baby in the home or an unsupervised TV receiver; of erratic familial sleeping habits. Sometimes the story is even grimmer. The family may be broken, embattled, hostile—and then the children's absences become excessive.

Whatever the story behind spotty attendance, unless a child is actually ill, he belongs in school where you can direct his learning.

As you study the attendance records, look for a pattern of absences. Look for the child who seems indisposed only in the morning; is habitually absent on Mondays and Fridays; is out on all holy days, regardless of religious persuasion; is inclined to become ill and absent in the afternoons; comes to school late and asks to leave early.

Six ways to improve attendance

If you find such attendance patterns, you circumvent them. When such an absentee returns to school, you tell him you missed him. You insist on a note from home and check on the signature. You phone his mother and express your concern for his health. You see to it that he gets make-up assignments for the work he missed, and you make doubly sure that he does them. You arrange exciting activities for Mondays and Fridays: trips, rehearsals, planning committees and reports. You set up Early Bird Helpers and include these reluctant students. *You don't let up!* And soon it'll be unnecessary to lavish so much attention on absentees, because they'll be coming to school and basking in your concern.

Then, when it's your turn to fill out attendance records in June, the story may well be different.

BEHAVIOR IS A PATTERN OF PERSONALITY

By all means, examine the confidential records of behavior that you will find among your files, but take them with a grain of salt. Children as well as teachers display varying styles of performance. Some children behave angelically in one room, outrageously in another. Some teachers record the veriest minutiae on the permanent records: Dick chewed gum in the schoolyard; Jack wrote notes to the girls. Other teachers, convinced that boys will be boys, make no note of such serious signals as temper tantrums, provocative teasing, in-fighting, or subtle and persistent defiance.

Since such records are subjective, no child should be tarred or whitewashed because of one teacher's entries. Over the years, however, the cumulative entries may indicate a pattern: Zelda is superficially compliant; Cindy is ultra docile; Maxine lies and tattles; Philip fights; and Jack attracts toys and money into his pockets. Whatever information you glean from the records will be helpful to you, although you may not always know how to handle the problems behind the obvious symptoms.

If you come on a problem that stumps you, discuss it with last year's teacher if possible, or with the guidance counselor. And, if the counselor is to help you, you will probably be asked to keep an anecdotal record of behavior of the troubled child.

An anecdotal behavior record is not a record of the teacher's judgment

You want these anecdotal notes to be of value to the person who reads them, so keep two criteria in mind when you write them up:

Make your notations representative of the incidents that occur: the good and the bad, the provocative and the negative.

Describe these incidents without bias or judgment. Write impersonally. Do not react. Do not interpret. Do not infer. Each incident noted should be a description of the child's momentary behavior, not of your outraged sense of values.

An anecdotal record is a recital of facts, not feelings

You may have to keep anecdotal records for Jeffry, an under-achiever who is a model of conformity; for Elvira, a braggart who cannot get along with her peers; for Frankie, who is overly defensive; for Eddie, who seems determined to bait you.

You may feel quite certain that Eddie's persistent and noisy tardiness is part of a plan to drive you to distraction, and perhaps it is. Your anecdotal notes will be helpful to the counselor if you indicate only the obvious facts, not your hidden feelings.

ONE EASY WAY TO WRITE UP A BEHAVIOR RECORD

Oct. 1: Eddie slammed open the door at 9:03 and said loudly, "Excuse me. The door was stuck. How am I supposed to get in if the door won't open?" He clumped to his seat, threw down his books, then went to the closet to hang up his jacket. Then back to his seat and back again to the closet to put away his lunchbox. He walked with a heavy tread, and when I asked him not to disturb the class, he sat down with elaborate quietude.

Oct. 2: Eddie came in at 1:05, with great excitement. "There was a dog in the schoolyard so I took him home because I know where he lives." Worked well all afternoon.

You continue your neutral observations, and record the variables as they occur. You may see genuine growth and effort. You may see glaring inconsistencies. Everything goes down on the anecdotal record for the counselor, who is trained to interpret.

Oct. 4: Eddie reported at 9:35 while the children were nominating the monthly slate of officers. Refused to participate or work.

Eddie absent all afternoon. Told the children he had more important things to do.

Oct. 5: At 8:20, Eddie was outside the school door when I arrived. Said he hadn't known it was so early, and anyway he had nothing to do.

Oct. 8: Absent all day. Seen riding his bike in the schoolyard. I did not send for him.

Oct. 9: Eddie waited for me again and so was on time. Worked fairly well but intermittently all day.

So written, your anecdotal records indicate a pattern. This one indicates the personality pattern of a boy whose clumping footsteps and slamming doors are cries for help. Together with the counselor's notations concerning the help that was given to him, the behavior record of this child, will indicate, at the end of the year, a problem noted, analyzed, and under guided observation.

And the next teacher who reads Eddie's record card will be more knowledgeable and understanding as she notes the facts of Eddie's behavior, rather than the feelings of his previous teacher.

SCHOLASTIC RECORDS ARE ONLY RATINGS

Most people think of a child's official ratings as achievement in the three R's, but this is a very narrow view of records. Scholastic achievement is not an isolated quality but is determined in great measure by a child's good health or lack of it, the regularity of his school attendance, the pattern of his behavior, and the attitude of his family toward education.

Two ways to make rating milestones meaningful

For proper grouping, you will need to assess each child's current level in terms of these additional factors: (1) chronological age, (2) potential.

Begin by checking out all birthdates. Children who are trailing the class in achievement may also be trailing the class in age. They may have been late entrants, non-English speaking, or in attendance only briefly. Or they may be very

194

young and in the wrong grade. Your knowledge of these facts will not automatically raise their scholastic ratings. Such knowledge becomes useful only after you've checked out their potential, because you can then devise catch-up plans that mean something.

To check out potential, you have to stop, look and listen, because official records will rarely help you in this respect. As realistically as you can, observe your children for the indicators of potential, which are the ability to comprehend; the ability to retain; the ability to use good work-study habits. If your assessment convinces you that the potential of a child or two or ten is remarkably low, consult your school psychologist, but engage in such consultations sparingly. Only about three to five percent of the school population is actually mentally retarded, so don't jump to the conclusion that you have a retarded group just because the level of achievement in your class is low. The underachievers who trouble you are more likely to be laggards of long standing.

If you find such laggards in your class, and every class has several, avoid these common pitfalls in dealing with them. Don't write them off, and out of the human race. Many geniuses were written off by their teachers: Einstein, Churchill and Edison were considered failures in school. Don't become sentimental saying, "Poor child—I'm so sorry for him. What can you expect? His home. . . ."

You'd be surprised how much teacher energy it takes to keep a child pegged out of the human race, or assigned to sentimental limbo! Don't do it. And don't settle for the old saw, "He does as well as can be expected." Does anybody?

If teacher energy is to be used, use it to release the learning power in your children so that you can push their achievement into line with their potential. And you can do this with two kinds of progress records: (1) your own class records, in which you keep a diminishing run-down of unlearned specifics so you can do something about them; (2)

your children's records, in which each child keeps track of and interprets his own indices of growth.

Then you put these records to work!

Devise class records that work

You may give the most carefully prepared lessons, but you have no way of knowing what academic information or misinformation your children have acquired *unless you check as carefully as you teach.* If you are the sanguine kind, you may be carried away by the sparkle of your top students. If you've had cause for embitterment, you'll be exasperated by the recalcitrants, and see little effort and more than a little tuning out of teacher. If you're the complacent kind, you'll conclude that Susie is a scatterbrain and needs to grow up; Johnny's really trying; Debbie was overrated by her last teacher; Bob is Bob and will never set the world on fire.

You cannot afford to be sanguine or embittered or complacent. You are a teacher with professional standards, and you know that parents expect high achievement, and taxpayers expect their money's worth.

No matter how capable you may be, your personal opinions will not give you a true picture of the learning in your room. And without a true picture, your best lessons may be reaching outer space instead of the inner space between the ears of your children.

Be realistic. If you teach on a high level, you owe it to yourself to check on a high level. Keep running records of your checking, and you'll be ahead of the game. You'll be able to pinpoint the weak spots as they occur in the learning of individual children, and, on occasion, in the class, and you'll be able to shore up these weak spots, and so get your children ready for the next level of work without being held back by the drag of cumulative misconceptions.

Make it easy for yourself to teach effectively, and make it possible for your children to learn effectively. Try developing your weekly plan in two parts, so that you have a teaching plan and a checking plan.

FOUR STEPS IN CHECKING ADD UP TO A PROGRESS RECORD

A good plan that will work for you and your children consists of a four-step checking triangle:

t-e-s-t-i-n-g and r-a-t-i-n-g
evaluating and analyzing
reteaching
retesting

With such a checking plan, you will find a considerable number of errors in Step 1. Then you'll find that the conscientious application of Steps 2 and 3 will reduce the errors in Step 4 to the *vanishing point!* Then you'll have, in effect, a record of progress! But the important thing to remember if you would truly see progress, is that these four steps are inherent in the day's work, and are part and parcel of a good learning situation.

Step 1: testing and rating

The only reason for giving tests is to obtain a score, a rating, a measure of achievement. Tests are, accordingly, designed to measure different factors. Some measure factual information, some measure learning skills, some measure application of learning. Tests may be short and informal, analytical, diagnostic, or long and comprehensive. Depending on your purpose, tests may be given at the end of a lengthy unit, after a single lesson, or even before you tackle a new lesson.

And every time you test, you get a measure of the child's

7777777777

achievement at that time: a gratifying 90, a distressing 40, a chronic 70.

If you find yourself being carried away by testing and measuring and recording, watch out! You may become a human rating machine, impersonal and not particularly effective. By all means, test and measure as a check on your children's academic learning, but remember that measurement by itself is only a static statistic without teeth. So enter your ratings of the formal tests as well as the informal quizzes into the record, and move right along to the second step to evaluate those ratings.

Step 2: evaluation

Evaluation puts the teeth into measurement because evaluation interprets the results of measurement. If yours is a wide-awake class operating on constructive individual and group skills, your children will see marks and evaluation as two sides of the same coin because: marks indicate the percent of achievement, measured according to the number of correct answers; and evaluation indicates the percent of error on the same test paper, as well as the quality of the specific error, meaning, for example, not a general error in capitalization, but a specific error with reference to capital *I*.

Suppose you're scoring this week's math test, in which you're checking on a lesson you've just taught—the bridging of tens. You find that Dennis achieved 80%, and so it stands to reason that he scored 20% in error. Focus on this 20%. He may grow up to be a carpenter and this missing 20% may cause his house to collapse.

On this same math test, you discover that other children missed these examples, too. You also find that several children stumbled on learning you had taken for granted—the addition of near doubles!

The first thing to do is to organize these errors in terms of their occurrence. The second thing is to spot the quality of error. So take a sheet of paper. List the names of the children down the left side of the page. List the examples across the top. Then, with a cross, indicate the examples missed by each of the children, and you will have a homemade, professional analysis sheet that looks like the table on p. 199.

You end up with two little groups, each needing clarification in one specific area of weakness: the bridging of tens, and the addition of near doubles. You realize it is time for Step 3.

Step 3: reteaching

This very important step is no big deal in time or effort. First, you call one little group to your desk, and then the other. To one, you reteach the bridging of tens, to the other, you review the addition of doubles and follow this with the reteaching of the addition of near doubles. And *presto!* The errors are gone! But you'd better make sure with Step 4.

Step 4: retesting

You may be convinced you've wrapped up these two little difficulties, but you'd better test your conviction by retesting the children. Give a brief, informal but exacting quiz to each of your little groups, and good! The children come through. Now give some special homework for reinforcement, check off your analysis sheet, and go on to the next piece of business in math.

If it should happen that two or three of these children don't catch on to your reteaching of a particular difficulty, don't scold, and don't nag, and don't give double homework, because it won't help. It *will* help to call them up again, and:

- Let each child analyze his error for you orally, then back up to the base that you see he comprehends, and work it out from there.
- Analyze your own teaching method of this particular item.
- Assign bright buddies.
- Try another approach.

Math Analysis Sheet

Date _____

TOPICS

| Names | Bridgings Tens | | | | | | | Addition of Near Doubles | | |
	#1– 9+3	#2– 5+9	#3– 2+9	#4– 7+9	#5– 9+6	#6– 6+5	#7– 8+7	#8– 7+6	#9– 5+4	#10 4+3
Dennis	x									
Bob		x			x		x	x		
Jerry		x	x			x		x		
Mark				x			x			

And then, a quick run-down of the four steps again, to certain success. You can't fail with the Four-Step Checking Triangle!

PROGRESS RECORD TECHNIQUES APPLY TO ALL CURRICULUM AREAS

In the same way, you can work this four-way checking and record-keeping technique into every area of your curriculum, and at different points in your timetable of lessons. And your efficiency will soon surprise you. Here are two learning situations that lend themselves to it: a remedial activity for phasing out ingrained misconceptions concerning the use of quotation marks; a jump-ahead lesson for checking out index skills.

Learning situation #1—a remedial activity phases out specific errors

If, at the beginning of the school year, you decide to develop a fifth or sixth grade written lesson in Creative Dialogue, you are certain to find that most of your children confuse indirect quotations with direct, and go completely AWOL in the matter of broken quotations. Some will bracket the names of people and places. Some will go so far as to decorate titles and captions with quotation marks. You will find their confusion in such a state of disorder that you will have to start from scratch.

Begin by planning your remedial strategy in three parts:

- Part 1 will involve the teaching and learning of indirect quotations.
- Part 2 will involve the teaching and learning of direct quotations.
- Part 3 will involve the teaching and learning of broken quotations.

And—you will make sure to follow each teaching activity with the four-way checking treatment before you move on to the next step!

When your children are thoroughly conversant with the use of quotation marks, they will be ready for another written lesson in Creative Dialogue.

This time, however, when your children engage in such a written lesson, your remedial efforts will show. This time you will discover very few errors in the use of quotation marks. Errors that are discovered, are again given the four-way checking treatment, and then—mission accomplished! Enjoy that glow of pleasure!

But all this takes time, lots of time. Remedial teaching is always time consuming, because you have to counter the tenacious and evanescent misconceptions that have become so firmly rooted in the children's heads throughout the years. Far better, don't you agree, to use your checking and recording techniques conscientiously in the first place, with new work?

Not only is this procedure effective in scouring out current errors as indicated in that math test that Dennis took, and in reclaiming old and ingrained errors by way of remedial instruction, but it is equally effective in getting the jump on new work.

Learning situation #2—a jump-ahead lesson checks out index skills

If you are planning a fourth grade unit based on research, you will save time and counter frayed tempers and enervating feelings of failure, if you check out your children's knowledge of the Reference Skills *before* you set them to the task of looking up material.

Follow the four-way procedure and insure happier working conditions for your class:

1. Give a detailed diagnostic test on the use of the index, on alphabetization through the third or fourth letter, and on cross references.

2. Analyze your test results. The class may already be proficient in some of these areas, but some children may

evidence many weaknesses. Get these weaknesses down on a homemade analysis sheet.

3. Clarify these weaknesses for your children, remembering that some of the errors noted may be due to the fact that the children had never been exposed to these skills, and other errors may be due to misconceptions. It may take a day or two, it may take a week or more, before all are proficient. When you think they are . . .

4. Retest to be sure—and then, knowing that your pupils are solid in this area, launch your unit with equanimity and—enjoy yourselves!

It may seem to you, that this kind of checking and record keeping takes inordinate time. With a little practice, it won't take any time to speak of, and you will have a record that is a Record of Academic Progress. This is a prime example of "Slow and steady wins the race." Then your children will indeed race ahead in their learning, but they will progress at different rates. Expect that. Some will learn very quickly; some will learn more slowly. But even your slowest child will show progress, and what he learns by way of this four-way checking technique will be virtually letter perfect, because this technique permits no hidden errors to become ingrained.

If you don't engage in this kind of checking and record keeping, your only alternative is wholesale teaching and re-teaching. And that takes more time, because you are then slowed down by a wholesale complement of built-in failure, compounded errors, and destroyed confidence. And there, you see, the syndrome for drop-outs is born!

Encourage children's records that work for them

As you engage in the good job of record keeping, and as you see the pace of learning quicken, don't keep this gratifying information to yourself. Share your findings with your children, because *they* are the ones who are being measured and evaluated. They have every right to know how they're doing, and they will be more receptive to learning if they know the score.

So allow them a say in the evaluative process, and involve them in personal record keeping. Immediately, they will get the feeling they are in business for themselves, and they will work with the same singleness of purpose as any man who's in business for himself.

Depending on your children and on your guiding hand, four kinds of personal records will keep each of your children in business. These are the planning records, quantitative records, qualitative records, and records that are purely personal.

CHILDREN'S PLANNING RECORDS

Children's planning records will include such personal notations as:

- What five things I need to work on in this class (and you won't have to tell Keith that he's weak in handwriting or in the multiplication facts concerning 12).
- What one thing I intend to make a splash in while I'm in this class (and this might be in a science fair project, in the development of a baseball skill, or in painting).
- What habit I intend to overcome because it gets me into trouble.
- What habit I'd like to acquire.

Planning records may be cooperative affairs, written and kept by a committee that may, for example, volunteer to develop a Surprise Bulletin Board. You will find that individual and cooperative plans are often outrageously ambitious. Your job is to help the children trim their plans to realistic proportions. And you do this in conference sessions where you help them organize their ideas and their timetables.

Quantitative records

The children's quantitative records will, to some degree, resemble your class records of academic ratings. Children may keep their ratings in columns, or for more visible pronouncements of progress, they may make their own graphs. Even little children enjoy making simple picture graphs, and older ones find the making of personal bar, line, and circle graphs, a spur to continuous success.

Qualitative records

The work folder is a kind of personal record that no child can quarrel with. Because it contains assorted test papers, reports, creative writings and maps, it's a tangible record of his work. Help your children keep this written work in neat, chronological order, by providing each of them with manila folders: one for the language arts, one for the social studies, and one for math. Help them further by periodically going through these folders with them, in your mutual search for evidence of progress.

You will find that the child who is keeping his own record of actual work will be propelled by the same spirit that propels the man in business, and he will do his best to succeed. Make certain, however, that the children understand these folders may not ever be removed from school, because you will need them so you can make your ultimate decisions in June—decisions that are fair!

Don't be surprised, as the weeks and months go by, to find that the work folders, on the whole, show evidence of increasing skill in functional activities.

The composition folders will very likely show two-way evidence of improved quality: in mechanics, meaning penmanship, neatness, paragraphing, and general punctuation; and in creative writing, in the use of vocabulary suitable to the topic, in the use of strong opening and closing sentences, and in the quality of expression.

The math folders will show evidence of phased-out errors.

The social studies folders will show evidence of increasing skill in written reports and in map making.

Personal records

These records will indeed be personal, and because they are, you must never break faith with a child in this area by divulging the nature of these "personals."

Start by asking your children to write about their personal feelings, and assure them that no one but you will see these papers. Ask them to write about such topics as "What I Like or Don't Like About This Neighborhood," or "What I Am Afraid Of." As time goes by, come up with other personal questions: "What I Expect of This Class" (and don't react if you read something not to your liking), "What Is Very Important to Me," "Things I Would Not Do if I Were a Grown-Up."

When children begin bringing you unsolicited "personals" you will know that you have indeed won their trust!

There are a number of benefits to children resulting from the keeping of personal records:

They learn to verbalize their formless feelings and, accordingly, get them out into the open.

They learn that a grown-up *can* be trusted.

They may even learn to like to write.

As a teacher, you will learn much about their secret inner lives. You will learn what troubles them, what stymies them, what motivates them. You will discover what enrages them and what leaves them cold. And, if you do nothing else, your sympathetic reception of these "personals" will break down some of the hostility against legal authority that so many children seem to nurture.

Children rarely hang on to records of their own contrivance once they move on to another class.

Teachers generally dispose of the day-to-day records in June, because they have served their purpose.

Only the official school records are on-going. And, when a teacher operates as you have operated, and puts these records to work, they will consistently show more than a fair degree of progress.

10

Increasing Parental Cooperation

You have finally mastered the course of study. You have finally developed good class control and pupil participation. You have even achieved skill in record keeping. Now you are asked to promote parental cooperation. And the idea is appalling!

If you are a young teacher, most of the parents are older than you. True, you are a professional, and you know about modern problems and techniques, but the wisdom that is to balance this knowledge is still in your future. In the meantime, you may be somewhat apprehensive and, in fact, a little afraid of the parents. Would you believe that many parents are more than a little afraid of you? And would you believe that some are too timid or too brash even to entertain the idea of cooperating with you?

Cooperation is a joint operation that involves understanding

According to Webster, *cooperation* is a joint operation.

In your class, parental cooperation is one part of this joint operation. Your cooperation is the other.

One of your colleagues might suggest that parents are a bore and a bother. She might warn you that parents can become a drag, or so domineering that they begin to tell you what and how to teach. At best, they might become a nuisance, using your time and your classroom for social or therapeutic reasons of their own.

This colleague will be speaking from personal experience—experience she found unpleasant and frustrating.

Your personal experience with parents can be pleasant and stimulating. And it will be, if you make it your business to understand their expectations, and see to it that they understand yours. And when you achieve this kind of understanding, you will be only a step away from that dynamic cooperation that sparks and boosts and supports learning power in your classroom.

Operation understanding is achieved in two steps

So here is a plan guaranteed to increase functional understanding between you and the parents of your children:

ONE WAY TO SYNCHRONIZE TEACHERS' AIMS
AND PARENTS' AIMS

First, clarify your thinking about your aims and the parents' aims. You want good, solid, sequential learning and constructive social growth for all your children. Splendid! What parents don't want the same things for their particular children? No quarrel here! The fact that quarrels and hard feelings occasionally do escalate between parents and teachers and local school boards, is due to a lack of communication that spells out these aims in a hundred personal and sincere and intriguing ways.

ONE WAY TO ESTABLISH COMMUNICATION
THAT COMMUNICATES WHAT YOU WANT TO SAY

For good lines of communication between yourself and the parents, your most carefully devised report cards are not enough. Your visits and talks with the P.T.A. are not enough. Your thank-you notes for kind rememberances are not enough. Communication is a broad two-lane highway with plenty of U turns permitting a rolling interchange of thoughts and ideas and expectations. Such an interchange, however, is easier said than done, if you are to use your daily five or six school hours to do the job you are paid to do, and that is to teach the children.

Guidelines for effective communication with parents

To be able to give your children every minute of your teaching day, and at the same time to derive the benefits of dynamic parental cooperation, you will need specific operating conditions:

YOU WILL NEED A 9 TO 3 FORCEFIELD AROUND
YOUR CLASSROOM OF "THERE-SHALL-BE-NO'S":

* *no* parental interruptions concerning helpful offers unless planned for in advance.
* *no* parental interruptions concerning an individual child's progress, absence, lunch or homework, unless the occasion is so serious that your principal asks you to stop teaching and confer with the parent.
* *no* parental social calls of any kind.

YOU WILL NEED PARENTAL INVOLVEMENT
IN DEVISING THIS COMMUNICATION
SYSTEM, MEANING:

* cooperative parent and teacher planning to help the class in general.
* cooperative parent and teacher planning to help individual children, specifically.

These operating conditions may now be very clear in your mind, but are they clear to the parents? Do they see your conditions as dictums of "There Shall Be No's" on the one hand, and "There Shall Be Cooperation" on the other? Remember that many parents are shy of you. Remember, too, that those democratic procedures which work with your children will work equally well with their parents in developing effective communication and mutual understanding.

Since you are the teacher, you will have to take the initiative in moving toward this mutual understanding. But you will have to plan realistically, and not merely with those winged words that moved you so poignantly in college. Do you recall those challenging phrases: "Every child is different"; "A teacher treats each child as an individual"; "A teacher releases the potential in every child"? Do you recall those stars in your eyes? And the stars *belonged* there! Nevertheless, in your beginning years, you may find what looks like an impassable gap between those winged words and the many children who seemingly don't care about their potential. But children do care, and you will find that their parents care even more.

This parental concern can work for you and your educational program *or* it can undercut your fondest dreams with stinging criticism. Actually, it is a mutual teacher-parent concern for children, so don't fight it. Don't fight the parents, either. Join them, instead!

A CLASS MEETING OF PARENTS WILL COMMUNICATE THE CLASS PROGRAM TO PARENTS

Join them and have them join you! Organize a class meeting of parents at the beginning of the term, when their interest in the new school year and the new teacher is high, and before you have any complaints to make to them. And to ensure success, announce a special social studies discussion for your children. Purpose? To consider the human resources in this community that could help us in our work.

Of course, you have the parents in mind, but you avoid saying or even implying that parents constitute a source of assistance in the community. Depending on their age, some children will view such a statement as all inclusive, some as sanctimonious. Other children, who have no parents or who are caught up in embattled homes, will align you with *them*, and write you out of their lives, too.

If you lead this discussion on human resources in our community with any degree of skill, it won't be long before the children will suggest that parents be invited to the class for a number of reasons.

At this point, make sure that you rule out possible hidden reactions in some of your children, which may prevent your relationship with the parents from developing on a high, operative level. Such hidden reactions may be quite touchy because they involve immature children who want their mommies to come and sit with them; independent, self-assured children who want school experiences reserved entirely for themselves; insecure children who may be embarrassed by the presence of their parents; and level-headed children who may consider parents an intrusion.

To avoid the possibility of such personal reactions, propose a group meeting at which nothing personal will be discussed about anybody. Make it clear that one of the purposes of such a meeting would be to discover those resourceful people that might, in some way, be of help to the class.

Now, might there be any other reasons for calling such a meeting?

*How to develop the reasons for calling
a class meeting*

Let the children discuss the possible reasons in class and at home with their parents. And the next day they will define the all-around purposes of a group meeting as well as any educational text, saying that their parents would have an opportunity to get acquainted with the teacher; the teacher could give the parents an idea of the class program for the coming year, of scheduled tests and report cards; the parents could see all the new books and materials the children are using; the parents could have a chance to ask questions.

Exactly! You couldn't have done a better job yourself, of spelling out the objectives of the meeting. But you wonder about those questions. You know that questions thrown at you from the floor may catch you unawares and rock you. A safe and helpful procedure is to collect these questions in advance. You do this by asking your children to interview their parents and bring back a list of three or four questions they want answered. Then you can group your questions in advance, and check on those you're not sure of. It could, however, happen that the parents shy away from asking questions of the new teacher, so here, for your consideration, are some questions that are frequently asked by parents:

- How much homework will you be giving?
- Will my child stay in the same reading group as last year?
- How can I help my child at home?
- Isn't going on a trip just a waste of time?
- Do you expect a book report every week?
- What is social studies?
- Can you explain the new math?
- Why do some teachers use films and TV instead of teaching?

How to plan your meeting in terms of four words

Once you are sure of your purposes and are armed with the answers to the questions that parents might raise, you are ready to set up your meeting. Again, plan it with the children. If they are involved, their enthusiasm will be caught by their parents who will want to come and participate. So plan this meeting with reference to four words: *place, time, preparation* (of physical surroundings) and *agenda.*

Place? The classroom, of course! Parents like to see the place where their children will be spending the year, so make sure that the room has a warm and lived-in look. And, since lay people are especially fascinated by the new instructional materials, have your maps and globes on display, your math and science equipment in sight, and your new attractive library books available for brief browsing. Do not forget to display the children's work. Although this is only the beginning of the term, get those papers and reports out of the desks and up onto the walls! (Caution! Don't display anything that is poorly lettered, untidy, incorrect or careless. A misspelled word, a misplaced capital, a rambling margin in a written report can be a source of acute embarrassment to a parent. It can also be a reflection on your standards at the very time that you are trying to sell your high educational hopes to the parents.)

Time? Tuesday, Wednesday, and Thursday seem to bring out more parents, but you will have to decide whether you want your first meeting to be held in the evening or in the afternoon. You will get more fathers to attend if you hold your meeting at night, but you will also run into difficulties with reference to getting the school building opened and heated and supervised. It is, on the whole, wiser to plan this first meeting for an afternoon, shortly after dismissal.

At this time, however, you will find that some children will also want to attend and that some mothers will want their children to stay with them, rather than to wait elsewhere. Since this is to be an adult meeting, you will find it running more smoothly if you restrict it to adults. If you permit or encourage children to be present, one or two distressing situations are sure to develop:

If the children are young, the meeting will hardly interest them and they will quickly become restless. Then, emboldened by the presence of their mothers, they will do what they would never dream of doing during your ordinary classroom activities: they will wander around the room; they will giggle and jostle and begin chasing each other; they will play with library books, unit materials and display objects. And when this happens, how will you be able to pull the meeting back to a professional level, when the mothers beam indulgently at their lively little boys?

If the children are older and you are counting on them to contribute to the discussion, you will be disappointed, because grade school children are so easily overwhelmed by a roomful of adults that they will quickly clam up. Then their mothers will become so busy sending piercing, wordless messages to their children urging participation, that they, themselves, will forget to participate in your discussion.

As you think about it, you see that your group meeting will be more productive if you confine it to adults. But you don't have to confine it 100%. One or two very small committees of your more mature children would lend a gracious note in welcoming parents, seeing that they sign the Visitor's Book, and escorting them to their seats. And a Reporting Committee could highlight some of the class plans for the year. They could tell about the plans to go on special trips, present specific assembly programs, engage in a science fair, and prepare class parties for seasonal occasions.

Once the meeting time and place have been set, you will want to think about invitations and other arrangements. You may want your children to write their own invitations, but you will find that parents invariably respond better to invitations written by the teacher.

Make this invitation as warm and personal as you can because you are the one, at this time, who is reaching out the hand of friendship, and you want that hand taken and clasped. Write your invitations neatly, observing all the rules of letter writing that you will be expecting your children to observe.

Here is a sample invitation that you will find helpful:

The Wingate Public School
25 Archer Avenue
Andover, Illinois

Dear Mrs. Hewitt,

This is to invite you and the other mothers of the children in my class, to a meeting on Wednesday, September 29, at 3:15, to talk about our new class and what we expect to accomplish. This will be an important year for Anthony. He is growing up and moving into all sorts of new activities, and I am sure you are wondering what these activities will be.

At this meeting, I would like to present an overview of the year's work. I would also like to hear from you and the other mothers about what you would like me to emphasize or introduce or reconsider. Your ideas will help me plan my work, and I will do my best to include them if I can.

Please come and spend the afternoon with us at our:

CLASS MEETING

Room 201 at 3:15 .... Wednesday, Sept. 29.

I look forward to seeing you then.

Sincerely yours,

Teacher, Class_____

Please tear off, fill out, and return.

I will attend the meeting_____
I will not attend the meeting_____

Signed_____(parent)

And here's a helpful hint! Although this is a warm letter, it is also a business letter, so the rules for handwritten notes do not apply. By all means then, make use of the duplicating machine in your principal's office. Remember to leave blanks for each child's name and you can fill in these blanks, later.

Delighted though the mothers may be to receive your invitation, some few will find it impossible to accept. Call each of these few on the phone just to say "Hello" and to tell her how sorry you are she will not be able to attend. Express the hope you will see her at the next meeting. Assure her pleasantly that you will be seeing her, at any event, at the individual conferences later in the term, when you will be discussing her child's progress with her.

Preparation with reference
to Physical Surroundings

Just before the meeting is scheduled to start, check the physical surroundings in your classroom:

- *Ventilation?* Yes, the windows are open.
- *Temperature?* Yes, the thermometer stands at a comfortable 70.
- *Housekeeping?* Yes, the shades are adjusted, the chalkboards are washed, the boards rubbers dusted.
- *Business techniques indicated?* Yes, sharpened pencils and sheets of paper are available for note taking.
- *Social set-up evidenced?* Yes, tables are pushed back and chairs are arranged in semi-circular rows.

And of course, you will have cleared this entire activity beforehand with your principal and with the school janitor.

Preparation concerning your agenda

Your meeting will last for about an hour, so plan to use your time judiciously. You will need about five informal minutes to get acquainted with the mothers, and if you prepare their name tags in advance, you will be able to match names with faces more easily. You will need two minutes to introduce yourself and to comment briefly on your background. You will need another 15 minutes to present your overview of the year's work, and to give the parents some idea of your policy concerning discipline and self-discipline. You will need an additional ten minutes to explain the use of your instructional materials. You will now have used up about half of your time. Take another ten minutes for answering questions, and if you keep to this timetable, you will have just enough time left to introduce the children on your Reporting Committee.

After the children describe the proposed highlights planned for the year, some of the parents will naturally volunteer to help with these trips and parties and plays and fairs.

Now isn't this exactly what you've been hoping for? So write down the names of the volunteering mothers, thank them warmly, and tell them you will call them a few days before each of these activities take place. And when you call them, plan to meet with them briefly in order to orient them in their responsibilities. It would never do, you know, to take four mothers along on a trip without their knowing what help you expected. If they don't know, they are likely to trail your class and to engage all day in personal observations. Five minutes of preventive orientation will save you hours of harassed concern on a trip.

Too soon, the meeting will come to an end. Take a moment when you thank the parents for coming, to express your concern that the short afternoon prevented you from hearing more from them. Indicate that you would like to hear more at another time. The parents will share your sentiments and move for another meeting. Excellent! Now do your best to move the focus of leadership from teacher to parents, because parents have a tremendous amount of concerned leadership locked up inside them.

And so, you set up the next meeting tentatively: a home would be a better meeting place than a classroom. An evening would be better than an afternoon because fathers could more easily attend. A pro tem planning committee needs to be appointed to develop an agenda. You need to stand by only as a guide, rather than as the dominating personality in the group.

Once you are launched on group meetings of this kind, you are launched on building parental good will and understanding, and then cooperation between you will become a functional fact.

But parents always work on two levels. In general, they are interested in the school and in the class program. In particular, they are interested in their own children, and "What have you done for my child lately?" is a natural parental attitude of inquiry. This being so, it would be wise to tell the group at the conclusion of your first meeting that individual conferences with parents will be scheduled within the next few weeks.

THE INDIVIDUAL CONFERENCE WITH PARENTS
WILL CONSIDER THE PROGRESS
OF INDIVIDUAL CHILDREN

You will be engaging in these individual conferences for a variety of reasons: because it's a school policy to report progress verbally to parents at scheduled periods; because a parent wants to see you concerning her child's difficulties in learning or behavior; because you want to see a parent concerning your difficulties in reaching her child in specific learning areas, or in guiding him in personal development.

How to get ready for individual conferences

In preparing yourself for an individual conference, ask yourself the same question the parents are asking mentally, "What are you doing for Timmy now?"

* Are you doing a great deal because he works hard?
* Are you doing very little because he's impossible?
* Are you doing an average amount because he's an average boy?
* Are you doing exactly the same for him that you do for the rest of the class?

It would be wise at this point to pause and reconsider your approach to your children. Certainly, it's human to become less than enthusiastic about a boy who is a truant and couldn't care less, or about a boy whose work habits are unbelievable and who never completes an assignment, yet manages to pass standard tests with flying colors. But such a lack of enthusiasm for his work pattern would only be reflecting his lack of enthusiasm for yours! You are the teacher, trained to reach your children, if not in one way, then in another. You do not write your problems off. You revitalize your professional concern, instead.

It is this professional concern that you will want to share with Timmy's mother at the individual conference that is scheduled twice a year, in most schools. And she will want to share her knowledge of what it is that makes him tick, with you. Together, and only together, can you both help Timmy to develop to his full potential.

So you write to your parents, indicating a schedule of open appointments. Ask each one to note a first and second preference of days and hours, and when they do, confirm the appointments promptly.

How to check out four preliminaries prior to the individual conference

Your individual conferences will move along smoothly and successfully if you give a little thought to these four preliminaries:

1. Discuss the forthcoming conferences with your children. Ask them what they think you should talk about. If they are second grade or older, ask each child to write you a confidential note indicating two strong points he would like you to discuss with his mother, and some one or two little things he knows he needs to improve in. If your children are very young, they can give you the same information verbally in a private little conference in class. You will find that most children, so approached,

see themselves quite honestly, and usually very correctly.

2. Post a DO NOT DISTURB sign on your door during the conference, so as to insure privacy.

3. Arrange to sit away from your desk during the conference. You will present less of an authority figure if you both sit at a small table.

4. Have the child's work folders of math, written expression and art, as well as his scrapbook and homework notebook, ready and available for inspection, so that the mother may have a chance to see samples of poor work and good work. (Have ready also some outstanding folders of other children, with their names covered, of course, just in case the mother has no idea of what is meant by good work at your class level.)

How to observe some important "do's" and "don't's" during the conference

So much for the preliminaries. During the actual conferences, you will want to practice some firm "Do's" and "Don't's."

Do set the tone. Be gracious, professional and enthusiastic. Say something complimentary about the child. Even if he's a tiresome child, his mother loves him for some reason. Find that reason and comment on it sincerely. You will then be meeting her on common ground and the meeting will be off to a good start.

Don't run down the child's learning background or imply criticism of his previous teacher.

Do be honest about the child's progress and be specific about his difficulties. If it's math, say he's having trouble with multiplying by eight and nine; with estimating distances; with the zero in the divisor in long division.

Don't say he's poor in math or has no head for numbers. This is too general and too devastating. There are 100 ways he might be hung-up, and 100 ways he could be helped. Indicate them!

Do practice the positive approach in your vocabulary. If a child is really troubled and troublesome, say he's:
—careless with the truth
—poor with respect to health habits
—not really trying
—showing little effort
—strong willed
—inclined to disturb the class

Don't use negative expressions. You will provoke defensive reactions in the parent if you say he's:
—a liar
—dirty
—lazy
—stupid
—stubborn
—a disturbing influence

Do listen. You will learn much from letting the mother speak, although she may tell conflicting stories. Be sympathetic. If necessary, assure her that everything she tells you will be kept confidential, if that is her wish.

Don't pry and *don't* argue.

Do write up the conference as soon as the parent leaves. If, during this meeting, you must make note of some statistical fact, show the mother what it is that you are writing.

Don't write during this period because that will make the mother apprehensive.

Do speak warmly and simply as you keep the conference going about this particular child, making sure not to compare him with other children or with siblings.

Don't use pedagogical double talk or words like emotional immaturity, aggression, cumulative records or percentiles. Such words are unfamiliar to most parents and constitute psychological accusations.

Do bring the conference to an end pleasantly and firmly after you: consider the help both of you will be giving the child (and remember that even excellent students need help if they are to work harder); review the points discussed; repeat the compliment you used at the beginning of the meeting.

Don't let the conference fizzle out on a note of meaningless small talk or social chatter.

Do see the parent to the door, invite her to keep in touch.

Don't dismiss her curtly.

Most interviews, so structured and so emotionally guided will be productive because the parent will leave with a glow of appreciation for her child's teacher, and the teacher will be left with an increased store of information about the child. With this information, you will then be able to plan his work more intelligently.

How to look at conferences that fail

But the most carefully planned conferences may fail because it takes two cooperating conferees to make a good conference, and sometimes you may meet parents who have problems of their own, or who are problems in their own right!

What would you do, for example, when confronted with a mother who:

- Damns the entire American system of education because "The schools don't teach their children to think."
- Says that you have enough time all day to teach her child and she doesn't want him burdened with homework because she wants him to play after school, or to take Greek lessons, or to practice the piano.
- Wants you to cut out such nonessentials as field trips, class newspapers, and assembly programs because she doesn't believe in permissive education!
- Decries your emphasis on skills mastery and discipline because it fosters rigidity of spirit.
- Is so overwhelmed by your educational background that she's convinced an invitation from you means trouble, and anyway, she's sure she has nothing worth saying.

How to work with problem parents

Of course, some parents are belligerent and hyper-critical, uninformed or excessively timid. They were that way long before they met you, so take no offense. Simply review in your mind your psychological guidelines for dealing with problem parents, and take it from there!

- Keep the interview on a pleasant tone. Don't argue. Don't become defensive. If necessary, agree that we all have a lot to learn.
- If the parent is extremely self-centered, verbal and critical, recognize it and comment on her ability to speak her mind. She will take that as a compliment. Good! Now put her to work and invite her to come talk to your class on a topic to be decided upon.
- Timid parents who are insecure need a few honest compliments such as, "How well your Susie behaves!

She shows her home influence every time we have
milk and cookies. Such nice manners!"

* And an extremely concerned parent who sees trouble
where there is none, needs reassurance from you because she has so many problems of her own. So reassure her. If all is well with Johnny, say so. If it isn't,
reassure her doubly by showing her how a simple
plan for help at home will really help him.

What to do after these conferences?

When the conferences are over and observations recorded on the cards, then what? Why, then you confer with
each child privately, and in a way report to him what happened during the adult conference. You did ask your children what it was they wanted you to discuss with their parents, didn't you? All right, then, tell them about it! And if
there's a plan of help, wouldn't it be silly to keep it to yourself?

Now you know

No matter how unapproachable, demanding, timid, or
indifferent parents may appear to be, the fact is they were
parents long before you met their children. And their concern for their children is real, although it may be hidden
under layers of impatience or sophistication, indulgence,
seeming neglect or argumentation.

This real concern needs continuous cooperative boost-
ing from you. Then with a little understanding guidance, this
concern is easily released and implemented on behalf of your
program in general, and on behalf of your mutual children,
specifically.

Now that you know how to do this—good luck!

11

Applying Regular Evaluation
To Insure Continued Learning

This was a good year

You've had a good year: busy children, creative activities, and a beautiful room. You've enjoyed the good will of the parents, the affection of your children, the respect of your colleagues. As for evaluation? A double plus!

Better make sure of that double plus. If you're really evaluating, you need to look not only to your emotional rewards, but also to your objectives.

EVALUATION? YOU NEED A DOUBLE BASE!

Since your objectives revolved around the release of learning power so your children could grow academically and socially, your evaluation techniques need to measure these areas in depth and to indicate the degree to which learning has taken place and the degree to which this learning is operative, is put into practice, and has become a way of life for your children.

Summarized into one sentence, your evaluation should tell you how effective you've been in helping each of your children achieve academically, *and* how effective you've been in changing their all-around behavior. If, for example, you've taught the mechanics of letter writing, can your children dash off a properly written letter to the mayor about the dirty streets in the neighborhood? If you've taught the basic number facts, can they hold themselves responsible for the weekly milk and lunch money in class? If you've taught health and safety rules, are they being practiced, or do the girls wear heavy sweaters in the classroom and open sandals on the gym floor; do the boys eat with dirty hands; does anybody leave bookbags in the aisle?

When you're evaluating your program, you want to measure the mastery of learning not only in the head, but also in action!

Knowing how enthusiastically you and your children planned the class program, how eagerly your pupils engaged in committee and independent work, and how scrupulously you followed up on your teaching, you feel you've done a good job. And so you have! But—isn't there a nagging doubt, now and then, that the class as a whole, dragged, academically?—That learning was occasionally spotty?—That concepts were sometimes vague, and skills acquired but not practiced? If these doubts are there, be of good cheer, because you are in the company of professionals. These conditions, in varying degree, exist in every classroom. That's because children come to school with different backgrounds, experiences, emotional drives, and mental capacities.

If you are truly on the way to becoming a professional, you will not say, "Because of their differences, these children are unable to respond to my best efforts."

You will say, "Maybe my methods are not varied enough to take care of these differences," and you will investigate additional methods and techniques. These you will try out and experiment with, as you strive to make your teaching day more effective.

But first, a look at your teaching day.

THE AVERAGE TEACHING DAY IS A THREE-WAY DAY

On an average day, you may find yourself engaged in three different but overlapping instructional activities:

- In *direct teaching*, as you present the development of a spelling rule, a number concept, a game skill.
- In *directional teaching*, as you participate in group planning sessions for the purpose of actualizing group skills.
- In *indirect teaching*, as you see to the establishment of habits and the inculcation of attitudes, by way of classroom routines, group interaction, and safety procedures.

If your year has indeed been happy and rewarding, you have only to look at your lively committees to know you have gone far in your *directional* teaching of participation skills. And you have only to look at your operating routines to know you have mastered ways of *indirectly* establishing habits and attitudes. The skills of *direct* teaching, however, are legion, and consequently take longer to acquire. That's because no single lesson stands by itself, but is, rather, one in a series of varied lessons. This series derives from your comprehensive teaching plan for comprehensive learning, which is, after all, your primary objective.

As noted in previous chapters, you have already devised exciting learning experiences. But do you know exactly what you did and how you did it? Could you do it again? Don't trust only to enthusiasm and good luck the next time around. Instead, check out the methods you've been using. See what they can and cannot do for a class!

METHODS STRUCTURE YOUR LESSONS!

If you are young, enthusiastic and dedicated, you've already adopted a number of methods as your very own. And wouldn't you say that you incorporated some of them into several structured lessons?

* There was the *appreciation lesson* that you used in literature to arouse enjoyment and admiration, and to stimulate extended reading. You've also used the appreciation lesson with powerful impetus in the social studies when you engaged class sympathies in the causes and struggles of a people, and sent your children off to the wonderful world of historical fiction.
* There was the *inductive developmental lesson* where you guided your children through the development of concepts in math and social studies. And you've surely discovered that nothing tops this kind of direct teaching for developing the scientific method, and for conducting organized but open-ended science activities.
* There was the *audio-visual lesson*. In this age of the multi-media, you've found that audio-visuals, including the texts, when used as aids to your teaching, provide reality to the studies of long ago and far away, immediacy to things too small to be seen, and special enrichment to lessons for children who are language poor.

No teacher could conduct an exciting program without these directed appreciation lessons, developmental lessons, and audio-visual lessons. Such lessons, in the hands of an interested and interesting teacher, sparkle and crackle, but by themselves may, nevertheless, lead to vague frustration and limited learning. That's because such lessons, no matter how spectacularly presented, are basically lessons in *motivation* for comprehensive learning. For your children to achieve comprehensive understanding in any segment of learning, they need to be involved in several additional kinds of directed lessons that give shape and form, continuity and wrap-up to your teaching. And these are: The Supervised Study Lesson, The Discussion Lesson, The Review Lesson, The Practice and Drill Lesson, and The Testing Lesson.

EIGHT LESSONS CONSTITUTE A STRUCTURED SERIES

You *don't* routinely put your children through eight directed periods of instruction, beginning with appreciation and ending with testing. But you *do* carefully structure this instruction in terms of eight directed presentations, and then, depending on the situation, combine them into three or four lessons, or extend them into three or four weeks.

And here's how you do it:

Suppose you are teaching a fifth grade and planning a small unit on "The Contributions of Science to Health." You might, then, begin your series of lessons with:

#1—An *appreciation lesson* concerning the discoveries of some of the great scientists: Leeuwenhoek and Metchnikoff, Jenner, Koch and Pasteur, and of course, Banting, Salk and Barnard. Combine this lesson, then, with . . .

#2—An *audio-visual lesson* in order to bring reality to the subject, and move right along to . . .

#3—An *inductive developmental lesson* designed to check on the work of Koch and Pasteur, whose great findings with reference to disease stemmed from their observation that bacteria multiply tremendously in the absence of scrupulous cleanliness.

Directing your children through the plan you used in your science lesson (p. 126), you start with the class aim: *To find out if there is any correlation between cleanliness, dirt, and the growth of bacteria.*

The *materials* will include half a dozen Petri dishes filled with sterile agar (borrowed from the local Board of Health) plus a bar of soap, running hot water, sterile paper towels, and the hands of a dozen children.

The *method* will call for a scrub-up session by this dozen. Then, using their right hands, four children will press their well-scrubbed finger tips onto the agar of dish #1, four others will do the same in dish #2, and the last four, in dish #3.

Twelve unscrubbed children may now be directed to press their fingertips, in the same way, onto the agar of dishes #4, 5, and 6. Then you cover the dishes tightly and store them in a dark cupboard for two or three days, after which time your children will be able to *observe, compare* and *come to a conclusion.*

But their most valid conclusions, no matter how exciting, will probably net your children only one bit of learning —that according to this experiment, there does indeed seem to be a correlation between dirt and bacterial growth. For greater depth and exploration of the original topic, you would be wise now not only to send your children off to study, but to engage them in . . .

#4—The *supervised study lesson,* in order to provide depth in learning by way of texts and references. In such a lesson, your children's aim would be to find out more about the men of science who worked on the prevention of diseases. Your aim would be to direct your children in independent study techniques and to satisfy yourself that because of previous instruction, they are now able to apply efficient ways of locating and abstracting knowledge; to use effective skills in organizing their findings on paper; and to practice constructive habits and attitudes in the use of their materials.

Make it easy for your children to demonstrate their knowledge of study techniques by making certain of these points: that the assignments are definite and easily understood; that the materials needed for study are plentiful, available and on a level with the children's reading abilities; and that you, moving about the room unobtrusively, are ready to guide some of the children in their immediate assignments; direct the brighter ones into more advanced avenues; and encourage the reluctant ones by helping them and/or adjusting their assignments altogether.

If, however, the whole class seems to grind to a standstill—stop! Analyze the situation and then proceed with step-by-step instruction in the technique that is stymieing them.

In a supervised study lesson, it is not enough only to direct your well trained class to read assignments and then to supervise that reading, because some children will attempt to memorize the veriest minutae, while others will gallop through the pages, snatching only at the highlights. What your class needs in order to get the most out of a lesson of this kind, is a simple, one-page Student's Study Guide that closely parallels the Teacher's Guide in your manual!

So study the teacher's guides that accompany your texts and adapt them for your children's use. Make these guides brief, basic, and broadbased enough for general use. Title them *Study Guides*, rexograph them clearly, and you will be doing your children an inestimable service as you direct them in supervised study lessons.

With or without a study guide, however, you'll be getting your children off to a good start in this kind of lesson by directing them to make up the best ten questions they can think of, for later testing.

And then you'll be ready to move along to the next directed teaching period, which is . . .

#5—The *discussion lesson*. This serves as a period for clarifying information. Testing for information, however, will have to wait.

For this lesson, you will want to have handy all those questions your children submitted, and you will want to use them as a possible core for discussion. But, first: review the art of questioning so you can make the most of the questions and the most of the answers; share this art with your children; plan to apply it by way of a committee, in order to start the discussion lesson with a challenge, keep it going in high gear, and end it on a lofty plateau.

How to use questions as teaching techniques

Questioning, as an art, is as important to teachers and children as it is to doctors and lawyers. There's much more to questioning than the asking of *who, why, what, when, where* and *how*. Handled skillfully, questions become high-level teaching techniques for directing attention to specific ideas in texts and graphics, current events and community living, as well as to salient features that are hidden within problems. A question can promote learning effectively, provided the *purpose* behind that question is simple, clear, easy to comprehend and within the ken of your children. Here are a few common purposes and sample questions—some very simple for your slower children, some more probing for those children who need only a challenge to be off and away.

Purpose: For specific recall.
Sample Q: Name five scientists who worked on bacterial diseases.
Purpose: For evaluating recall.
Sample Q: Which scientists do you consider most important in the conquest of bacterial disease and why?
Purpose: For comparing people, ideas or things with regard to one particular feature.
Sample Q: Compare Leeuwenhoek and Koch with regard to their use of the scientific method.
Purpose: For comparing people, ideas and things in a general way.
Sample Q: Compare the 19th with the 20th century scientists.
Purpose: For relating cause and effect.
Sample Q: Why did bacteria flourish so luxuriantly in some Petri dishes and not in the others?

Purpose: For analysis.
Sample Q: Describe the qualities that characterize a scientist.

Develop this matter of purpose behind questions with your children. Direct them in making up specific questions based on specific purposes and then get them to analyze the purposes behind the questions in texts and on printed tests. Your children will learn to ask questions that crackle. But —this will happen only if you restrict the learning at this time to the art of the *asking* of questions, not to the answering.

After such experiences with questions, your children will want to classify the dozens of questions that have grown out of the supervised study lesson, and they'll want to elect a committee to head the discussion lesson, which is next in your teaching plan. Such energetic ambition!

CAUTION! The idea for a question may be triggered by a wonderful purpose in mind, but it may be so poorly framed that it will fail to achieve anything of value. So here are some "do's" and "don't's" that apply to the *wording* of questions:

Re the wording of questions

Do, when you are emphasizing specific factual learning, word your question in such a way that the answers are almost automatically equally specific, e.g., When did Leeuwenhoek invent the microscope?

Don't word the question so it can be answered with a simple *no* or *yes;* e.g., Did Leeuwenhoek invent the microscope? And *don't* be so vague in questioning that the answers are scattered; e.g., What about Leeuwenhoek?

Do frame questions so they will necessitate some thinking; e.g., What's the difference between bacteria and germs?

And *don't* fall into the leading question abyss; e.g., After whom was the process of Pasteurization named?

Soon your children will be convinced that they know how to frame questions in terms of particular purposes. Good! Then ask them to react to, and reword, some questions which you know are poor, both in purpose and in wording. Here are a few such questions:

> *Poor question:* What do you think about pasteurization and how do you think people reacted to it 50 years ago when we know how important it is to health?
>
> (*Comment*): A pupil wouldn't know which of the two or three questions he was expected to answer.
>
> *Reworded question:* How does the public attitude toward pasteurization today compare with the public attitude of 50 years ago?
>
> *Poor question:* What do you think about scientific journals?
>
> (*Comment*): A vague question!
>
> *Reworded question:* What kind of information do you expect to find in scientific journals?
>
> *Poor question:* What did we do before pasteurization?
>
> (*Comment*): Who is *we* and to what does the word *do* refer?
>
> *Reworded question:* How did people keep their food edible before pasteurization?

If you and your children know the techniques of wording questions effectively, you also need to know and to practice the techniques of *steering the questions* in such a way that real and worthwhile discussion takes place during your discussion lesson. Then the questions will serve to clarify information, which is the basic aim of your discussion lesson!

Such clarification of information, however, isn't automatic, because there are pitfalls—enticing and tempting pitfalls. But expert teachers steer their questions around such pitfalls as:

- Repeating a question. NEVER! If some children seem not to have heard you, ask another child to repeat the question.
- Repeating an answer. NEVER! To make sure that answers are audible, keep moving about the room, away from the child who is speaking. He will automatically raise his voice so you can hear him—and so will the rest of the class.
- Asking questions from a prepared list. NEVER! This practice tends to deaden discussion. Of course you and your committee will want to have your questions prepared in advance, but play them out by ear.
- Calling on pupils in a fixed order, alphabetically, by desks or tables. NEVER! This makes for a mechanical kind of procedure, and puts the emphasis on marks rather than on free and vigorous discussion. And don't call on a pupil first, before you state your question. If you do, the rest of the class will tune you out. It is far better to state the question first and then call on someone for the answer.
- Making a practice of questioning only the brightest and most eager students. NEVER! Draw out the quiet and the shy ones by asking: Do you agree with the last statement, Tommy? Why? How would you defend Janet's statement? Could you back it up, Eric? If what Mario says is true, what might happen next, Juliet?
- Asking too many questions during a period. NEVER! This is a bird shot technique that makes children nervous and tense. It throws the burden of moving the activity onto the teacher and it permits little time for the children to react to the question, think through the answer and express themselves with any degree of facility.
- Minimizing the importance of children's questions. NEVER! A good lesson is characterized not only by

the question a teacher or a committee throws out, but it is also characterized by the bubbling questions that children raise and the comments that they volunteer spontaneously.

Although a rousing discussion is grounded in questions, don't make your period look like the situation depicted in Figure 10.

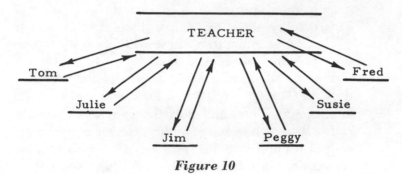

Figure 10

Make it a point, rather, to develop the steering technique whereby a good question can be kept going among the children for four or five minutes. Launched by a good question, the discussion, for example, may start with Tom and then move on to Jim who challenges Tom's answer—then on to Peggy who supports Tom—to Julie, who interjects doubt—to Frank, who defends Julie's position. Then your pattern of discussion will look like that represented in Figure 11.

Only with well framed and purposeful questions, and with considerable care in the steering of them, will you be able to stop dominating your discussion lessons. Then you'll be able to exchange domination for guidance, and thereby release the thinking power of your children. When that happens, your discussion periods will sound like heated town hall meetings.

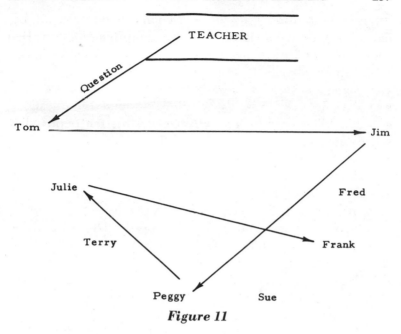

Figure 11

CAUTION! Questions may be excellent, discussions heated, and your class electrically alert, but you will still need to check on the breadth of your children's learning, in terms of the topic they're on. And for this, you need . . .

#6—*The review lesson.* A review lesson is a *new-view* lesson, meaning that you now use another approach to the material under study, and you do this to ensure learning from another point of view, in the event that the first approach did not "take" with some children; and to enrich learning and make it multi-faceted.

Since it's the scientists and their contributions your children have been studying, what better review could you have than the establishment of a Hall of Fame! Suggest it. Have the children set up a committee of five or six scientists and their assistants, give them three days to gather more material for reports on "My Life and My Work," and be prepared for pictures, posters, placards, and a star studded panel! And, of course, you will assist this committee in planning, so they come through with flying colors.

Only two more lessons and you will have completed your series of eight in your structured plan for comprehensive learning!

#7—*The practice and drill lesson* for fact fixing and speedy recall must satisfy two psychological basics:

Practice must be correct if learning is to be correct. If, for example, your children are practicing the spelling of Pasteur, it would do them no good to write it five times, if they misspelled it five times.

Drill for specific facts must be speedy if recall is to be speedy. For this topic, surely the names of the scientists, their achievements and the application of their achievements to today's health problems should be so much a part of your children's learning that recall, without groping for the answers, should become virtually automatic.

To insure responses that are speedy and correct, you will periodically need to engage your children in suitable games, bees and flashcards. Devise these activities in such ways that time is used economically and efficiently. And here, for example, is how you can do exactly that, with teacher made flashcards, so as to get *total pupil response* every time.

Suppose you wanted to fix a dozen matching facts in the minds of your children. You wanted to be sure they knew exactly which scientist was responsible for which achievement. So you devise a good sized 5″ x 15″ card that looks like this:

1)	2)	3)
Pasteur	Koch	Barnard

You hold up your card and ask, "Which scientist was responsible for heart transplants?" Since the answer is Barnard, who is #3 on the card, you will expect each of your children silently to raise three fingers. Had you asked, "Which scientist discovered the tuberculosis germ?" you would have looked for two raised fingers.

Using cards in this manner, you can, with one glance, note instantly which of your children needs further clarification with respect to any particular fact. You make notes of such facts for later follow-up, and prepare more cards as you need them.

Suppose you wanted to fix facts with reference to sequence of time. Then you would make up cards that looked like this:

1)	2)	3)	4)
Heart transplant	Pasteurization process	Invention of microscope	Insulin for diabetes

And you'd ask: Which was developed first? Which last? Which preceded the last? And—each time, you'd get a class response by way of raised fingers—speedly, total and silent, instead of one audible answer from one child.

Such periodic drill cycles will keep the facts from slipping away. With an increasing store of facts, the children will engage in discussion periods with increased depth. And, powered by such depth, the end-of-the-year test scores should top all expectations.

To make sure that your children score what they deserve in all areas of the curriculum, initiate them into the so-called mysteries of test making and test taking. And you do this whenever the checking of facts is called for: before a lesson, after a lesson, in mid-unit or at the end of a unit; and a good time to begin is with . . .

#8—*The test lesson.* Used as a lesson, a test will reward you and your children with much information concerning class weaknesses and strengths. Then you will be able to plan for specific improvement that is needed by specific children, and you will be able to see where your teaching efforts are least needed. All of this calls for using such precise techniques in testing that your tests become instruments of precision, as carefully devised as your most carefully structured lessons. And for this, you need to be aware of 3 V's:

- There's the V for *vocabulary*. Since every curriculum area, in fact, every unit of work, has a vocabulary of its own, make sure that your children know it before you plan to test them on it. Even bright children may fall down when computing problems in math if they don't know the precise meaning of such terms as sum, total, divisor, product, quotient. In the same way, they may know how to answer a question when it's worded in one way, but not in another. What would your children do with this one question, worded in three ways?

    The opposite of rich is old, strong, poor, wealthy.
    To be rich means the same as: old, strong, poor, wealthy.
    Rich refers to: old, strong, poor, wealthy.

    Unless your children are familiar with the vocabulary, they tend to stop at the first word they recognize and to check it without reference to the question!

    There's the V for *vitality*. There's no reason why a test need be an instrument of dullness or torture. Tests can be almost as exciting as a good discussion period, and but one step removed.

    This one step refers to the depth of questions asked. For oral discussions, you want questions that children can open up and keep going, because you want them to clarify their information. For written tests, you want questions that are short and well framed and call for short exact answers because you're testing information that was supposed to have been acquired. Do this by vitalizing your questions, varying the format of the tests, and removing fear and tension from your children.

- And there's the V for *variety*. Tests may be varied so they are long or short, subjective or objective. They may be based purely on factual recall or on the thoughtful analysis of given facts. They may be taken with desks cleared or with textbooks open!

When you and your children want to check on study habits and group participation skills, on projects, reports and trips, subjective tests of one kind or another are generally used, depending to a great extent on personal reaction and opinion. Sometimes you do the subjective rating by observation. Sometimes your children check themselves subjectively, on class-constructed tests of behavior traits, work habits, personal weaknesses and progress.

When, however, you and your children want to check on the degree of academic learning in the subject matter areas, you usually construct written tests. Most common among the written tests are the essay test (not often used because it calls for some subjectivity in rating), and the short answer tests. It will pay you to be scrupulously objective about this kind of testing and to work it out with your class whenever you can.

How to Make Tests Interesting and Profitable: Favorites among the objective tests are the short answer types which are easy to devise, easy to take, easy to score, and easy to analyze for diagnostic purposes. And so, here are some of the short answer types, together with sample questions relating to assorted curriculum areas:

> *Enumeration Tests:* List five words that you can make up with the prefix *ad.*—List five combinations of numbers that add up to six.—Name three com-

munity workers that stand ready to help you in your neighborhood.

Completion Tests: The Revolutionary War began in _____ and ended in _____. The first landing on the moon took place in _____. The sum of 3 and 4 and 5 and 6 is _____.

Multiple Choice Tests: Circle the correct answer for—To build a house on the coast, you hire sailors, carpenters, tailors.

True and False Tests, also known as *Yes and No Tests, or Right and Wrong Tests:* A day is 12 hours long _____. Three fours are more than two fives _____. A city is the same as a village _____.

Reasoning Tests: We use stoves in the kitchen because 1) they belong in kitchens; 2) they get hot; 3) they help us cook our food. *Or:* People turn on lamps at night because 1) lamps have switches; 2) lamps give light; 3) lamps are decorative.

Association Tests: These are used to pinpoint the connection between two facts such as cause and effect, dates and events, cities and states, synonyms and antonymns. This kind of test frequently calls for *matching;* e.g., draw lines between the related items in Column 1 and Column 2 below:

Column 1	*Column 2*
Albany	cars
Rome	New York
Detroit	earthquakes
San Francisco	religion
Las Vegas	lobsters
	gambling

Although it's possible to make up a simple, short answer test using only true and false or association questions, it's much more challenging to make up a composite test which includes all kinds of questions. Then your test will be calling for answers that need to be enumerated, selected, or reasoned out! All on the very same topic! So let the children help you devise such a composite test. Announce the topic and ask half a dozen committees each to select the type of test they particularly like, and to work up ten appropriate and properly framed questions. Then all you have to do is to choose the most interesting five in each category, and there you have it—a rollicking, readymade 30-item test! Now you set it up in an organized manner, rexograph it, and it should look something like this:

Class Test on the Topic of _____

I—Questions for Enumeration

      1—
      2—
      3—
      4—
      5—

II—Questions for Multiple Choice

      1—
      2—
      3—
      4—
      5—

III—Questions for Completion

      1—
      2—
      3—
      4—
      5—

IV—True and False Questions

      1—
      2—
      3—
      4—
      5—

V—Reasoning Questions

1—
2—
3—
4—
5—

VI—Association Questions

1—
2—
3—
4—
5—

When, in addition to continuous subjective evaluation, you involve your children in this kind of ongoing objective testing by asking them to make up challenging questions, you provide unremitting practice in the art of questioning. Then it becomes possible for them to view questions and tests as varied and purposeful learning techniques. When they can see that, they'll be ahead with the answers. They'll also be on your side when it comes to diagnosing errors and rectifying them. Then, when the day of reckoning comes, the day of the city or state or national tests, your children may not know all the answers, but they will know how the questions were devised, what they call for, and how they should be answered. And that constitutes a lot of learning!

All this will be happening in your room because you've been concentrating on educational action:

- You've released the learning power in your children by involving them in exciting and meaningful experiences.
- You've used selective methods to insure effective teaching and independent learning.
- You've devised tests and utilized them as teaching techniques to find out if your children were learning what you thought you were teaching.

- And you didn't let go!

Success Formula for Educational Action

Whether you're aware of it or not, you've been following a simple, hard-to-beat formula that adds up not just to mastery of learning, but to *mastery in operation,* and this formula consists of:

- one part cooperative planning and teaching
- one part released learning power that is leashed by directional study techniques
- one part personalized evaluation
- one part objective testing.

With this formula, you can't fail!

And that's it. Now you have the techniques you need to release the learning power in children, and you're looking ahead to meeting your new class in September. But before you do, consider these questions:

What classroom procedures would you continue to use in the same way, and why?

What will you be doing differently and why?

What will you stop doing and why?

What will you try to do that you hadn't tried before, and why?

Then formulate your answers in terms of your children, your personality, your dedication and drive. Devise effective methods of your own to release your teaching power. And follow the Success Formula. It works!

Index

Please remember that this is a library book,
and that it belongs only temporarily to each
person who uses it. Be considerate. Do
not write in this, or any, library book.

SEA DRAGON HEIR

Copyright © 2000 by Storm Constantine

A Tor Book
Published by Tom Doherty Associates, LLC
175 Fifth Avenue
New York, NY 10010

www.tor.com

Tor® is a registered trademark of Tom Doherty Associates, LLC.

Design by Lisa Pifher

Library of Congress Cataloging-in-Publication Data

Constantine, Storm.
    Sea Dragon heir / Storm Constantine—1st ed.
        p.   cm.
    "A Tom Doherty Associates book."
    ISBN 0-312-87306-9 (alk. paper)
        I. Title
PR6053.O5134 S43 2000
823'.914—dc21

                                                      99-059314

First Edition: March 2000

Printed in the United States of America

0   9   8   7   6   5   4   3   2   1

This book is dedicated to Deborah Jayne Howlett, my incomparable friend, whose humor and love have brightened my life for many years.